MOUNTAIN MEN

Volume 4

True Tales of the Old West

by

Charles L. Convis

Illustrated by Mary Anne Convis

PIONEER PRESS, CARSON CITY, NEVADA

Library of Congress Catalog Card Number: 96-68502

ISBN 0-9651954-4-9 (Volume)
ISBN 0-9651954-0-6 (Series)

Printed by
KNI, Incorporated
Anaheim, California

CONTENTS

ILLUSTRATIONS

DEADSHOT DAREDEVIL

Robert McClellan was noted for athletic ability and speed. Once he leaped over a team of oxen, rather than walk around them. He was also one of the best marksman in the country.

Before he became famous in the Oregon fur trade, McClellan scouted for Mad Anthony Wayne, fighting Indians after the American revolution. In 1794 Wayne sent McClellan and two other scouts out to capture a live Indian. They found three roasting venison on high ground in an area free of brush. The scouts crawled, undetected, to within two hundred feet of the Indians' fire.

"I'll rush them when you shoot," McClellan whispered. He laid his rifle down and took a sprinter's stance.

McClellan charged forward as the other scouts fired. Two Indians fell dead, and McClellan reached the third before he could pick up his weapon. He pinned the Indian to the ground, holding him until the other scouts came up. They bound their captive and led him back to General Wayne.

A few weeks later McClellan and three companions, acting solely from a spirit of daring, dressed and painted like Indians and rode directly into a group of warriors, gathered around a campfire. Within arm's length before their disguise was discovered, they fired their weapons and rode away in a hail of bullets. The Indians captured one scout and executed him the next day. McClellan, wounded, escaped.

Some say McClellan was the first American to trap on the Missouri River. It was in 1801, two years before the Louisiana Purchase. If any earlier trappers were American, history doesn't identify them.

McClellan was going up the Missouri River in 1806 when he met his friends, Meriwether Lewis and William Clark, returning from their discovery expedition. McClellan provided a bottle of wine (probably the explorers' first in three years) and the three men talked over their days of campaigning together against Indians in the East.

In 1810 McClellan became an original partner in Astor's Pacific Fur Company. By that time he was described as one of the "finest shots in America. With a keen eye and a steady hand, he was brave as a lion."

In January, 1812, McClellan reached Astoria in present Oregon with the first group of trappers to travel overland from the United States. On that journey McClellan's marksmanship in shooting a bighorn sheep at a critical time saved his party from starving.

He was in the return party two months later when 130 Indians attacked, as the trappers portaged around The Dalles. McClellan then performed feats of athleticism and marksmanship unmatched in the history of the West.

One of his companions described McClellan's response to the Indian attack:

"Had not McClellan, with a bravery and presence of mind peculiar to himself, leaped dexterously over a canoe, he would have been felled to the ground; but his agility saved him, and in all probability saved the whole party, for he instantly shot the man who aimed the blow, then drawing a pistol from his belt, shot him who had assailed Reed dead at his feet; then clapping his hand to his mouth, in the true Indian style, he gave the war whoop, fired his rifle, and the Indians fled."

The Indians, panic stricken by the leaping, shooting, yelling white demon, ran as fast as they could.

Some time later McClellan wanted to show an Indian what a white man could do with a rifle. He set up a board with a two-inch bullseye. From one hundred yards away, he fired three bullets through the bullseye. Then he pushed a hazelnut into one of the holes, stepped back again one hundred yards, and shot two bullets through the nut.

McClellan died in St. Louis in 1815. His old friend, William Clark, brought McClellan's body to his own farm for burial. It appears that Clark arranged for the tombstone which reads:

> To the memory of Capt. Robert McClellan. This stone is erected by a friend who knew him to be brave, honest, and sincere; an intrepid warrior, whose services deserve perpetual remembrance.

Indians, both east and west, learned that Robert McClellan was no man to trifle with.

Suggested reading: Alexander Ross, *Adventures of the First Settlers on the Oregon or Columbia River* (New York: The Citadel Press, 1969).

A PROMISE KEPT

The first Americans Lewis and Clark met on their 1806 return from the Pacific Coast were Joseph Dickson and Forest Hancock. Dickson had settled on the Mississippi River, across from St. Louis, where he took up trapping. When Lewis and Clark stopped nearby to spend the 1803-04 winter, Dickson got excited about following them to trap upstream on the Missouri.

"Forest," Dickson told neighbor Hancock, "I'll bet those soldier boys will see some right smart beaver country. Let's you and me foller them. This Mississippi's gittin' plumb trapped out."

Hancock agreed to go.

The two men trapped the 1804-05 winter near the mouth of the Platte, operating out of a cave they had dug into a hill. They got many furs, but Indians stole them all.

They tried again the next winter, but Sioux blocked their way upstream. Dickson was wounded during an ambush. Again, Indians stole their furs.

In spring 1806, they got past the Sioux and reached the friendly Mandan villages, where Lewis and Clark had spent the 1804-05 winter. Dickson and Hancock received the same friendly treatment from the Mandans that the explorers had enjoyed earlier.

On August 11, 1806, paddling upstream near the mouth of the Yellowstone, Dickson and his partner met Clark's group coming downstream. The next day they met Lewis and his group. John Colter, with Lewis, persuaded his captains to give him a discharge so he could turn around and go back to the mountains with the two trappers.

Dickson and Hancock were delighted to have Colter join them.

"He'll show us some real beaver country, Forest," Dickson said, smiling.

Somewhere along the Yellowstone, the three stopped for the winter. Colter and Dickson had a fierce argument. When the air cleared, Colter and Hancock traded for an Indian canoe and moved away, taking most of the supplies. Dickson was left alone.

The 1806-07 winter was a hard one, with unusually deep snow. Constant exposure to bright sunshine on fresh snow finally blinded Dickson. Until then he had not been a religious man. Convinced that he was going to die, Dickson knelt and prayed for deliverance.

"God," he prayed, "if you will spare me, I'll be a faithful Christian for the rest of my life."

When Dickson got to his feet, a strong feeling came over him that he should take the inner bark from a tree near the entrance to his cave, grind it, mix it with water to form a poultice, and put it on his eyes. He followed the mysterious directions. When he went to bed with the poultice on his eyes, he did not know whether it was day or night.

When Dickson woke, his eyes felt better. Eventually he recovered his full eyesight. He had a successful spring of trapping, and headed downstream with a large canoe-raft of furs.

Dickson traveled through the Arikara and Sioux nations by moving at night and hiding by day. But he was almost killed one morning when an Indian suddenly stepped into the river and grabbed his canoe. Another Indian on the bank raised his rifle to shoot. Dickson, acting instinctively, jerked the first Indian toward him just as the second man's rifle fired. The bullet meant for Dickson killed the first Indian. In the excitement Dickson got away without injury.

When Dickson reached St. Louis, he sold his furs for several thousand dollars. He had been away from home for almost three years. He learned that he now had a fourth child, two and a half, named Joseph for him. He and his wife would have five more children. He named the next one Missouri Dickson in memory of his remarkable trip.

Dickson never forgot his promise. One of the first things he did on his return to civilization was to be baptized and join the Methodist church. He moved to northern Illinois and farmed. He donated part of his land to the church. He was the principal organizer of Zion Chapel in Sangamon County.

"Joseph Dickson is one of the best stewards I ever saw," said a Methodist circuit-riding preacher.

No one could doubt that the trapper had faithfully kept the promise he made during that horrible winter alone on the Yellowstone.

Suggested reading: Frank H. Dickson, "Joseph Dickson," in LeRoy R. Hafen, ed., *The Mountain Men and the Fur Trade of the Far West* v. 3 (Glendale: Arthur H. Clark Co., 1966.)

TWO MEN WHO LOVED THE MOUNTAINS

Army privates John Colter and John Potts met and became good friends in 1803, when they volunteered for the Lewis and Clark Expedition. Colter, a 29-year-old Virginian, enlisted just to join the expedition. A shy man, Colter's pleasant expression reminded many of Daniel Boone, then enjoying his old age in Missouri. But the fire burning in Colter fed on danger. Potts, two years younger, had already been in the army three years. But he missed the dark, forest-covered mountains of his native Germany, and he looked forward to seeing more of them in America.

On its return from the Pacific Coast in 1806, the expedition divided. Potts and Colter went with Captain Lewis. They traveled overland past the great falls of the Missouri River, and explored the Marias River. On the Marias they killed two Blackfoot Indians who were trying to steal their horses. These were the only Indians killed on the three-year expedition.

After Lewis's party resumed its downstream journey on the Missouri, they met two trappers coming upstream to look for beaver. The trappers persuaded Colter to ask for his release from the army so he could join them. The captains both agreed, provided no other soldier asked for his discharge until they reached St. Louis. Potts, who also wanted to join the trappers, reluctantly told his friend goodbye.

"I vish mit you, John, I can stay," Potts said. "Das land back dere sure nice ist."

"Maybe we can hunt it together sometime."

When the expedition reached St. Louis, a grateful congress awarded each enlisted man a 320-acre land bounty. It was not enough to keep John Potts away from his beloved mountains.

The next spring he joined another expedition, led by Manuel Lisa, and headed back up the Missouri River to trap beaver. When they reached the mouth of the Platte River, Potts was delighted to see his old friend coming downstream in a canoe.

"Had a falling out with those other two," Colter said. "Decided to head back for the settlements."

"Vee going up to beaver trap," Potts said. "Tell Lisa if another mon vee need."

Manuel Lisa was delighted to get a man of Colter's experience. Colter turned his canoe around and headed upstream. Potts moved to his friend's canoe to help paddle. The expedition traveled up the Missouri and Yellowstone Rivers, stopping at the mouth of the Big Horn. There they built a headquarters fort and started trapping.

6

Lisa wanted Indians to come to the fort and exchange furs for trade goods. To reach as many Indians as possible, he sent Colter on a remarkable trip, covering what is now Yellowstone Park and the Montana-Wyoming-Idaho area surrounding.

Colter explored the sources of the Big Horn, Wind, Green, Snake, and Yellowstone Rivers. He crossed Jackson Hole and the Tetons, and followed around and through present Yellowstone Park, back to Lisa's fort. He was the first white man to see the important features of Yellowstone Park.

Potts kept trapping with Lisa's men. He missed his friend that winter. When Colter returned in spring 1808 with momentous stories of steam erupting from the earth, of bubbling tar pits, and fire and brimstone fountains, Potts and the other trappers listened in wonder. But they did not doubt the stories, for they knew that John Colter spoke the truth.

Later that summer Colter was an unwilling participant in one of the largest inter-tribal Indian battles in history. Three hundred Crows and five hundred Flatheads fought fifteen hundred Blackfeet. Colter, fighting with his Crow friends, was wounded. The Blackfeet, seeing the white man helping their enemies, remembered the killing of their two tribesmen two years before. From that time on, they were implacable enemies of whites.

That fall Potts was glad to be back with his friend trapping beaver. They paddled their canoe up the Yellowstone River, portaged over Bozeman Pass, and went down the Gallatin River to the Three Forks of the Missouri. Then they paddled up the westernmost fork, the Jefferson.

Remembering the battle earlier that year, Colter kept a wary eye out for Blackfeet.

"We're in their country," he warned Potts. "Better keep your eyes peeled."

"Mein John, no worry. Like the eagle from the tall tree, I watch."

About six miles from the forks, five or six hundred angry Blackfeet warriors suddenly confronted the trappers from both banks. The Indians' signs made it plain the canoe was to come directly ashore.

"There's no way out of it, John," Colter said. "They probably just want to rob us. I'll drop the traps to the bottom and we'll go ashore."

"Old hoss, in der minds more den robbing ist. Out in der vater, mein chances I take."

Colter, realizing that escape was impossible, quietly slipped the traps into the water and moved the canoe toward the shore.

When the canoe touched the bank, an Indian seized Potts' rifle. Colter stepped out of the canoe, wrenched the rifle away, and handed it back to his friend.

As Potts pushed off into the stream, an arrow thudded into his chest. He cried out, "Mein John, bad hurt I am."

Potts killed the Indian who had shot him, and then slumped forward into the bottom of the canoe. Immediately, dozens of arrows struck his body.

As Colter watched his friend die, the Indians stripped him naked and grabbed his rifle. After a quick council, the chief signaled for their captive to "go away." Colter, expecting a lingering death by torture, did not understand.

He started walking, thinking he would be shot from behind. But the chief shouted and made signs for Colter to run. Then the captive saw the young warriors stripping off blankets and leggings as though preparing for a race. Some picked up lances or axes, watching the chief for a signal. Then Colter understood the deadly game about to be played. His life would be the prize.

As the mountains looked down on the drifting canoe and its lifeless occupant, Colter broke into a run and heard hideous war-whoops behind. The Madison River lay six miles east, across a plain covered with prickly pears. Colter pushed his naked body to its limit. He dared not look back, but he thought the war-whoops sounded fainter.

When he reached the height of land between the rivers, his nose started bleeding. Blood gushed out on his chest and abdomen. Then Colter looked back and saw that he was far ahead of all the pursuers but one.

Colter stopped and spun around as the Indian approached, his lance raised to strike. The warrior lunged, and Colter wrenched the lance from his hands. The warrior lost his balance and fell. Colter pinned him to the ground with his own weapon.

Colter sped on to the Madison. The yelling warriors were out of sight when he rushed down to the stream. He plunged through willows and cottonwoods, diving under a pile of floating driftwood. He found a place where he could keep his face above water and still be hidden.

For the next two hours the Indians searched. Sometimes they stood just above Colter, and he wondered how they could miss him. He promised God that if he escaped he would never come back to Indian country again.

After the warriors left and darkness fell, Colter swam silently down the river for a considerable distance. Then he crawled out and traveled overland the rest of the night. It took him seven days to reach Lisa's fort, 250 miles away. The other trappers did not recognize him. His beard was long, his naked body emaciated by hunger, and his feet swollen and sore.

By spring Colter was thinking of the traps he had left in the Jefferson River. Forgetting his promise to God, he set out to recover the traps.

Colter had camped on the Gallatin Fork, near the Jefferson, when he heard leaves crackle behind him. He leaped over his cooking fire, scattering sparks and coals as arrows whistled past. He climbed to the top of a high cliff and hid. Again he promised God that if he could only escape once more, he would leave the Indian country for good. When it seemed safe, he returned to Lisa's fort.

The next year Colter had another narrow escape from Indians back in the same Three Forks country.

"God," he prayed, "if you'll only help me out once more, I'll leave this country the day after tomorrow. And damned if I'll ever come back into it again."

He kept the third promise. Colter headed downstream in April, 1810. He returned to Missouri, married, and settled down near the retirement home of Daniel Boone.

Colter lived three more years — years filled with thoughts of his friend and his own miraculous escape from the Blackfeet.

Suggested reading: Burton Harris, *John Colter, His Years in the Rockies* (New York: Charles Scribner's Sons, 1952).

THE WIND OF DEATH

George Drouillard, son of a French-Canadian father and a Shawnee Indian mother, was in his twenties when he signed on as interpreter with Lewis and Clark in November, 1803. His pay would start the following spring.

George, an eager young man, hoped he would be allowed to hunt and scout as well as interpret. His chance came early. In July, 1804, one of the soldiers deserted. The captains ordered Drouillard to follow the deserter's trail.

"Bring him back, dead or alive," they ordered.

Drouillard brought the man in, alive. By then, Drouillard's hunting skills had made him the expedition's leading meat-getter.

Drouillard's greatest service came in summer 1805, when he found the Shoshoni Indians in the Three Forks country of present Montana. Lewis and Clark knew the Indians would be suspicious of the white expedition. The first contact would be critical.

"If we see them before they see us," they told Drouillard, "we'll have a chance to meet in peace. If they see us first, they'll likely run or fight. Then we won't be able to trade for the horses we need to get across the mountains. You need to see them first, George."

"I'll do my best."

Drouillard found the Shoshonis and signed that the explorers came in peace. But for his work, the expedition might never have reached the Pacific.

Drouillard also showed his hunting skill after the explorers met the Shoshonis. The Indians had been out of meat for a long time. Drouillard killed three deer. The grateful Indians, some near starvation, even ate the entrails and the soft parts of the hooves.

When the expedition returned to St. Louis in September, 1806, Drouillard received $833.33 for his service of almost three years.

The next spring Drouillard joined a fur trading expedition, led by Manuel Lisa. They started up the Missouri River to reach the Rocky Mountains. Lisa soon considered Drouillard his right hand man.

When the expedition reached the mouth of the Osage River, Antoine Bissonette deserted. Lisa sent Drouillard after the deserter with orders to bring him back, dead or alive. Again, Drouillard brought in his man. This time, however, he had to shoot Bissonette to capture him. The prisoner was wounded too seriously to continue on the journey; Lisa sent him back downriver in a canoe.

Lisa's party continued up the Missouri and Yellowstone Rivers and built a fort at the mouth of the Bighorn. Drouillard made two long journeys from the fort, looking for Indians from whom they could buy furs.

In August, 1808, Drouillard returned to St. Louis. Arrested as soon as he stepped off the boat, Drouillard learned that Bissonette, the deserter he had captured the previous year, had died on his way downstream. When Manuel Lisa found out that his right-hand man faced murder charges, he posted a $5000 bond and helped Drouillard hire three of the best defense lawyers available.

The trial was held in St. Louis. George Shannon, youngest man on the Lewis and Clark Expedition, served on the jury. One wonders why the prosecutor left him on, as Shannon always looked up to Drouillard and had spent many hours with him, learning to hunt.

The summations of the defense lawyers took over three hours. They contended that the killing was justifiable because the victim had deserted the expedition. They also contended that their client was only carrying out valid orders. The jury took fifteen minutes to return a not-guilty verdict.

Drouillard went back up the Missouri River the next spring, wintering again at Lisa's Fort. In spring 1810 he and thirty-one other trappers moved west to the Three Forks country and built a fort there.

That May Drouillard was trapping with two Shawnee Indian scouts when a party of Blackfeet attacked. The trappers were only a short distance from the fort, clearly within hearing range on a normal day. However on this day a brisk spring wind blew away from the fort.

When his friends found Drouillard's body, they realized that but for the wind they would have heard the shooting and come to his rescue. Drouillard, using his horse for a breastwork, had fought stubbornly and long. The number of empty cartridges was mute testimony of his valiant resistance before he and his scouts were overrun.

George Drouillard was killed near the place where he had so distinguished himself — as a hunter, as a scout, as a negotiator — just five years before.

Suggested reading: M. O. Skarsten, *George Drouillard, Hunter and Interpreter for Lewis and Clark* (Glendale: Arthur H. Clark Co., 1964).

WHEN BEAVER FUR CAME HIGH

The year after Lewis and Clark returned from their expedition with reports of beaver on the upper Missouri, Ezekiel Williams joined twenty other men to go up the river, seeking fortunes in trapping.

Beaver were many, and trapping was good. The men returned the next season and talked of crossing the mountains to trap on the Columbia. But in 1810 a hundred Blackfeet warriors attacked, killing five of the trappers. The survivors built decoy fires and slipped away. They rode twenty-four hours before resting their horses. They escaped to the land of friendly Crow Indians. One man stayed behind and married a Crow woman. The other fifteen continued south, planning to trap on the headwaters of the Platte.

Soon after the trappers reached the Platte, hostile Indians stole all their horses. Williams led six men in pursuit. Sixty Indians attacked. Only Williams and one other survived.

With no horses and five more men killed, prospects for the ten remaining trappers were bleak.

"I'm afeared the thieves will take our horses to their tribe and bring back more men to rub out the rest of us," Williams said. "We better hide our plunder and skedaddle."

Working rapidly the trappers cached their furs in a dense growth of brush. Then they hurried on south, traveling now on foot.

When the trappers reached the next large river, they split up to trap along its headwaters. The next spring, after what Williams called a "wretched winter," all but three had been killed by Indians. Those three did not agree about where they were.

"I say it's the Red River," Williams said. "We kin float downstream to the Mississippi."

But Jean Champlain and the other — named Porteau — thought they were on the Arkansas and should travel southwest to reach Santa Fe.

"I'll find white people or lose my scalp trying," Williams insisted. "You kin look for Mexicans if'n you want."

His companions helped Williams build a canoe. They cached their furs and said a tearful farewell on March 1, 1812.

They were, in fact, on the Arkansas River. Williams trapped as he traveled downstream. He met a Spaniard who directed him to some Spanish settlements. He cached his furs and went to the settlements for the winter. He heard nothing about his former companions.

In spring 1813 Williams returned to the second Arkansas cache, picked up his furs, and continued down the river.

In June, after he had taken a hundred more beaver skins, Williams was captured by Kansas Indians.

He took an active part in tribal life, and fought with his captors against their enemies, the Pawnees. For his distinguished service in their war, his captors set him free but kept his furs. Williams reached Cooper's Fort on the Missouri River in the fall.

Williams talked to Indian Agent George Sibley, who delivered annuities to the Kansas Indians.

"They tuk my furs," Williams complained. "Treated me fine otherwise, but I want the skins back."

Sibley agreed to withhold annuities from the Indians until they returned the furs.

In May, 1814, Williams joined a group of men leaving to trap on the Arkansas. When Williams reached the distant place where he and Champlain and Porteau had cached their furs, he asked local Indians about his former companions. They told him they had heard from the Crows that the two men had been killed.

Williams and three companions built bull boats from buffalo skins and waited for the spring rise in the river to float the cached furs downstream. There was little snow in the mountains, and the river rose slowly. While Williams and his companions waited, they were captured by Comanches. Again, Williams and his friends escaped. They hid until the river had risen enough that they could start downstream with the furs.

About five hundred miles downriver, they were again stopped by low water. Williams cached the furs again and walked north to Boone's Lick, Missouri. He heard during the winter that a rival fur company planned to steal his cache, so in spring 1815, accompanied by two young boys, Joseph and William Cooper, he returned to the cache on the lower Arkansas. He had the furs back on the Missouri by late summer, and he sold them for five thousand dollars.

Eight years had passed since Williams had started trapping. He did not try to recover the cache left on the Platte. He felt he had already paid too much for the furs he did get to sell.

Suggested reading: David H. Coyner, *The Lost Trappers* (Glorieta, New Mexico: Rio Grande Press, 1969).

KIT CARSON'S FIRST "INDIAN"

Kit Carson, a legend in the West, is mentioned in shelves of books. This story seems to appear in only one.

Christopher Houston Carson was born in Kentucky on Christmas Eve, 1809. When he was one year old, his family moved to Missouri. On their way, they passed a cabin where Nancy Hanks nursed a boy, just a few months older than Kit. That boy grew up to save the Union that Kit would do so much to expand.

The Carsons settled near Daniel Boone in Howard County, Missouri. When Kit was fourteen a falling tree killed his father. Kit apprenticed out to a saddle and harness maker in Franklin. He did not like the work. He would rather listen to stories about adventures in the mountains. He ran away at sixteen to be a mountain man.

In August, 1826, Kit asked Charles Bent if he could join Bent's wagon train to Santa Fe.

"Kin ye shoot?" asked Bent, looking at the long flintlock in the boy's hands.

"Yes sir," replied Kit. In fact, the sixteen-year-old was already an expert shot, one of the best in Missouri.

"Kin ye stand guard?"

"Yes sir."

"Hev ye got a blanket?"

Kit's face fell. "I reckon I don't need one."

Bent found the boy a blanket and a tin cup. He let him join the train.

The long string of twenty-eight wagons, each drawn by eight mules, impressed Kit. The train also included smaller, ox-drawn wagons as well as Delaware Indian hunters, mountain men, the captain and his crew, and mounts for all. A rag tag herd of spare animals — lame oxen, extra saddle horses and mules, untamed ponies, and mares with foals — scrambled along in the dust at the rear.

"You'll ride at the rear," Bent told Kit. "Don't let 'em straggle too fur behind."

Kit rode a mule to wrangle the untamed mob of reluctant animals, most of whom tried to return to Missouri pastures. He ate with the mountain men, and listened, spellbound, to their tales. They told of friends getting rubbed out by Kiowas at a big rock near the great bend of the Arkansas. They told of hiding their furs on the Yellowstone to escape pursuing Cheyennes, and losing their horses to Comanches on the Staked Plains.

Kit learned to rope stubborn mules, keep strays in line, and persuade tired oxen to get back on their feet and keep moving. He learned to sleep on the hard ground in spite of mosquitos, thunder storms, and stamping animals.

In two weeks the train reached Council Grove, the beginning of the real plains. Now they had to watch for buffaloes and Indians. There, Kit's guard duty began — four hours every third night. He learned to stand just outside the corralled wagons, his loaded flintlock in his arms, his eyes and ears alert for the slightest sign of an Indian.

When they reached the great bend of the Arkansas, the mountain men killed several buffaloes. The next day, a half dozen Pawnees tried to stampede their animals. That night they reached Walnut Creek. They laid over a day to amputate the arm of an injured man.

Two more days brought them to the big rock, a landmark as famous as Independence Rock would later become on the Oregon-California Trail. The tall rock on the Arkansas, between Walnut and Pawnee Creeks, marked a disputed area where Indians fought with each other for hunting rights. All Indians agreed, however, that white men would not be allowed.

The night they reached the rock, Kit had guard duty. Thoughts of the bloody amputation and a countryside filled with hostile Indians filled the boy's mind as he stood his watch.

They posted Kit at the foot of the rock. Others went to the top, and some stood guard at a distance. Just before midnight, someone yelled "Indians." A rifle shot was heard. In a few minutes Kit came running into the wagon corral.

"You see any redskins?" someone asked.

"Sure did," Kit answered. "I kilt one of the red devils, too. Saw him fall."

The rest of the night was quiet. At the first streak of daylight, everyone was up to see the boy's dead Indian. They found Kit's own riding mule. He had shot the animal squarely between the eyes.

Later that day the Pawnees did attack. The battle lasted three days. It was the battle that gave Pawnee Rock its name.

Kit remembered the battle with a rueful grin. But he never said much about it.

Suggested reading: Henry Inman, *Tales of the Trail* (Topeka: Crane & Company, 1898).

KIT CARSON AS A YOUTH

Colorado Historical Society

JAMES P. BECKWOURTH

Colorado Historical Society

CROW COURTSHIP

Jim Beckwourth liked to exaggerate. The life story he gave his biographer contains too many thrilling escapes, too many scalped Indians, too many stolen horses to be completely true. It amounts to mythology, but a mythology based on fact. Beckwourth really had the thrilling adventures; his numbers were just too big.

Like many whose lives needed no embellishment, Beckwourth tailored his overstatements to the stories. In one story, probably with little exaggeration, he tells of courting one of his many Crow wives in the early 1830s.

Red Cherry, the most beautiful woman in the village, already had a husband. But Big Rain, while subject only to the head chief, performed only domestic duties and earned little respect from the village braves. Many of them plotted to win Red Cherry away from her proud lord. Beckwourth took a more direct approach.

"I went to Big Rain's lodge," he said. "I was painted to the extreme. His lady reclined on her couch, half asleep. I strode in and laid my hand on her brow.

"'What do you want here,' she said.

"'I have come to see you because I love you.'

"'Don't you know I belong to the chief?'

"'Yes, but he does not love you as I do. He never goes to war, but idles in the village. I am a great brave, and always go to war. I can paint your face and bring you fine horses. As long as you belong to Big Rain, he will never paint your face.'

"'My husband will kill you.'"

Beckwourth's father had been a major in the Revolutionary War, his mother a slave. A man of mixed races, Beckwourth chose to live as a Crow Indian. He would become a head chief of that nation. When he wooed Red Cherry, he was just a warrior, but a true, red-blooded one. Later he would interrupt his Rocky Mountain adventures to fight in the Seminole War in the East and in the California Rebellion in the West.

Beckwourth left Red Cherry's tipi with her ring on his finger. The next day he led a raid against the Blackfeet. Upon returning, he sent a message to Red Cherry:

"We'll elope after dark. Tell me where to meet you."

The lovers honeymooned on a horse-stealing raid against the Blackfeet. Big Rain fumed when the raiders returned with many horses. He and six of his sisters inflicted a horrible beating on Beckwourth. The victim fell to the ground, enduring the beating with Indian fortitude.

"If I had resisted," Beckwourth said, "they would have been justified in killing me. But if they had drawn just one drop of blood, I would have been allowed to take their lives. They laid it on so unmercifully that I became angry and hoped they would draw blood."

One of Beckwourth's wives scolded him for stealing a married woman when so many eligible maidens in the village would have been willing to move into his lodge.

"I told her I wanted the handsomest woman in the village for my lodge," Beckwourth said.

After celebrating with a horse-dance, Beckwourth led another party to raid the Blackfeet. Again, Red Cherry slipped out of Big Rain's lodge to join him.

After four days the raiders returned with three scalps. Again, Beckwourth was seized and flogged by Big Rain and his sisters. When the beating ended and Beckwourth's wounds were dressed, one of his wives presented him with a new-born son.

"He will make as great a brave as his father," she said, proudly. "His name is Black Panther. Here, look at your child."

In 1855, when Beckwourth told his life story, that son had become the head counselor of the Crow Nation.

Two nights after the second beating, the persistent Beckwourth and Red Cherry, accompanied by many warriors, made another raid for Blackfoot horses. On his return Beckwourth got his third beating.

After that beating some of the warriors who had followed Beckwourth went to Big Rain.

"You have whipped him three times and you shall whip him no more," they said. "Red Cherry loves him, and she does not love you. You can turn the Bighorn River uphill to its mountain sources before you can separate them. We will buy your claim to Red Cherry and give her to Red Arm for his own. You, a great chief, should despise to want a woman who loves another warrior better than you."

Big Rain dropped his head, for he also loved Red Cherry. But he reluctantly accepted the offer. He resigned all interest and title in Red Cherry for one war horse, ten guns, ten chief's coats, scarlet cloth, ten pairs of new leggings, and ten pairs of new moccasins.

Jim Beckwourth had another wife in his crowded lodge.

Suggested reading: T. D. Bonner (ed.) *The Life and Adventures of James P. Beckwourth* (New York: Alfred A. Knopf, 1931).

GRIZZLY HUNTING

When George Belden first saw the magnificent grizzly and her two cubs in the pine-covered foothills of the Bighorn Mountains, he knew he had to have her. Her skin would draw many compliments from admiring, jealous friends. He waved and shouted to his hunting partner, La Frombe, and their Santee Sioux guide:

"Follow this way. I'll ride around and cut her off."

Belden assumed the bears had a den in the brush-filled ravine ahead. He spurred his horse past the animals and fired a shot, hoping to turn them back and give his companions time to catch up.

He dismounted, tied his horse, and walked back, cautiously watching for the bears. The sound of cracking brush broke the stillness. Belden looked up and saw the bears on a ridge, high above.

They had passed him. He heard his horse snorting in terror. Then it broke free and crashed through the heavy growth, dragging the tie-rope behind. Belden hoped the bears would follow the horse back into range, but they just sat on the ridge and watched.

Belden moved back into the undergrowth and hid behind some shaggy pines, blown down by wind. Several minutes went by. The bears, probably thinking he had left, came back down the slope until the mother was within range.

Belden could not yet see his companions, but he decided to shoot, anyway. He aimed his Henry rifle at the mother's heart and squeezed the trigger. Although Belden would one day outshoot Buffalo Bill Cody in a rifle match at Fort McPherson, this shot only wounded the grizzly.

With a roar that shook the hillside, the mother bear crashed to the ground and rolled over. She got back on her feet in an instant, her blood-red eyes fixed on her assailant. Belden's heart sank as he faced the enraged animal. He could almost smell her rotten breath as she roared her defiance. The cubs crouched to watch, and their mother started toward her attacker. Belden fired again but missed the mother, hitting one of the cubs.

The cub screamed; the mother turned and ran back. Belden pumped three more shots into the retreating bear. She turned from her wounded cub, lurching back toward Belden. He fired again into the cub, who again cried in agony. The mother was just a few feet from Belden when, unable to "withstand the piteous cries of her cub," she turned and went back to lick the cub's wounds.

Again Belden shot her; again she whirled toward him, and again he shot her cub. By the time she retreated from the scene of battle with her cubs following – one of them very lame – the mother had been hit thirteen times.

La Frombe and the Santee rode up while Belden was deciding whether to pursue the bears or leave well enough alone. He directed his mounted companions to head off the bears while he caught up. Running as fast as he could, Belden reached the wounded cub. He killed it with one shot. Then he backed away to watch. The mother came back, sat by the dead cub, and "howled most piteously."

In Belden's words:

"Then she took her paw and rolling him over and over, shook him as if to wake him. Smelling his nose, she seemed to understand he was dead, and cried as if her heart would break. Suddenly she saw me, and, standing on her hind feet, looked at her persecutor. She made no attempt to come at me, but seemed to be waiting for her death. Never did I see so magnificent a beast, as she stood there, with ears flattened against her head, her eyes blazing like coals of fire, her neck stretched out, and her mouth wide open, disclosing four rows of immense white teeth. I did not long keep her in suspense, but fired at her heart, and she fell down and rolled over, catching her cub, and seemingly trying to embrace it as she died."

They skinned the mother bear and loaded her hide and the dead cub onto a packhorse. They started for their temporary hunting camp. A war party of about fifteen hostile Crow Indians rode into view. The hunters dropped the cub to lighten their load, and rode for their lives. They knew they had trespassed into Crow hunting grounds.

The Indians pursued until they saw the hunters' camp. Not knowing how many men were in the camp and fearing a decoy, they turned and rode off. Belden and his companions broke camp at dark and rode all night.

They were fifty miles away by sunrise.

Suggested reading: James S. Brisbin, *Belden, the White Chief* (Athens: Ohio University Press, 1974).

THREE BOATMEN IN THE MOUNTAINS

Mike Fink was probably the oldest man to answer the Ashley-Henry advertisement in 1822 for a hundred enterprising men to go up the Missouri River and trap beaver. At fifty-two, he had already become a legend. Younger men who would become famous in the mountains — Jim Bridger, Jedediah Smith, Hiram Scott — looked at him in awe, wondering if they could ever measure up to his reputation.

Mike had learned to shoot by hunting squirrels near Pittsburgh, where he grew up. He always won his quarter of beef at local shooting contests. Eventually they bought him off from entering the contests by giving him the hide and tallow for staying away so other men would have a chance.

Totally fearless, Mike gave up scouting and Indian fighting to become a boatman on the Ohio. Each boat had its champion, who had won his laurels in saloon brawls, drunken revelries, and frontier fighting contests. The red feather a champion wore in his cap challenged the champions on other boats. Mike was recognized as the champion of all the waterways from Pittsburgh to New Orleans.

Mike's jokes were sadistic, and his rough and tumble fighting vicious. He was reported to have loved and left women in countless Ohio and Mississippi ports.

"I'm a Salt River roarer," Mike would shout, as his keelboat entered a port. "I love the wimmin, and I'm chock full of fight."

With no more men to accept his challenges and no more women to accept his favors, Mike may have become a mountain man out of boredom. Two of his close friends, Bill Carpenter and Levi Talbot, answered the same advertisement, and they all went up the Missouri together. Mike had trained Carpenter and Talbot. Their daring and shooting skill closely matched his.

The three ex-boatmen, in a party of about sixty trappers, stopped for the winter near the mouth of the Yellowstone River. There they built a fort for protection from Indians, and they trapped nearby streams. Mike and his friends preferred to live outside the fort. They fixed up a cave in the river bank and lived there.

Sometime that winter, Mike and Carpenter had a terrible quarrel, reportedly over an Indian woman. On a visit to the fort in spring, Mike started drinking, and memories of his trouble with Carpenter returned.

"Let's make us a peace treaty, Bill," Mike said.

"How's that?"

"Let's each put a cup of whiskey on our heads and let the other one shoot it off."

"Who goes first?"

"You pitch a copper and we'll see."

Mike won the coin toss and the right to shoot first.

Bill must have known Mike's intention, as he made an oral will leaving everything to Talbot before he faced Mike with the cup of whiskey on his head.

At a distance of sixty yards, the man who had been the best shot in the Alleghanies drew a bead. Then he lowered his rifle and grinned.

"Hold your noggin steady, Carpenter," Mike shouted. "Don't spill the whiskey, I'll want some in a minute."

Mike hit Carpenter dead center in the forehead, about an inch and a half above the eyes. He lowered his rifle, coolly blew smoke from the touch hole, and shouted again as Carpenter slumped to the ground, dead:

"Carpenter, you done spilt the whiskey!"

Mike claimed the killing was an accident, and the other trappers allowed him to go free on that basis. Even though Talbot knew better, his long friendship with Mike kept him from saying anything.

But a few months later, Mike carelessly bragged to Talbot that he had killed Carpenter on purpose. Talbot immediately drew the pistol he had inherited from Carpenter and shot Mike Fink through the heart. The rip-roaring, half man-half alligator, always chock full of fight boatman fell to the ground dead.

A few weeks later Talbot distinguished himself fighting Arikaras in the bloodiest battle the mountain men ever had with Indians. Shortly after, he drowned in the Teton River.

The three old boatmen weren't in the mountains long, but they were something to watch while they lasted.

Suggested reading: W. Blair and F. Meine, (eds.) *Half Horse, Half Alligator* (Lincoln: Univ. of Nebraska Press, 1981).

TOUGH OLD BEAR HUNTER

Hugh Glass, old gray-bearded hunter from Pennsylvania, was with the Ashley-Henry 1823 expedition to the Rocky Mountains when eight hundred Arikaras attacked. The Indians killed twelve trappers and wounded thirteen, including Glass. Some of the survivors marched up the Grand River in present South Dakota, bound for the Yellowstone country. They wanted to build a fort at the mouth of the Bighorn and trap beaver the next season.

Glass, brave as a grizzly bear and tough as \whang leather, was an expert shot.

"I want you in the lead to hunt for meat," Major Andrew Henry said.

Grizzly bears loved the Grand River Valley and its dense berry thickets. The Arikaras loved to hunt there, so Glass watched carefully.

On the fifth day in the valley, a female grizzly, protecting her cubs, suddenly attacked Glass. He fired one shot before she ripped his throat open and tore a mouthful of flesh from his thigh. Glass tried to regain his feet, but she pounced again. For a few terrifying seconds she raked his body with her claws and crunched her fangs through to the bones in his hands, arm, shoulder, and back. Then the bear, weakened from her wound, collapsed.

Agonized screams brought Glass' companions running. Shocked at what they saw, they needed no doctor to tell them the chances of survival. With frightful wounds in his scalp, throat, chest, face, back, shoulder, arm, and thigh, they wondered how Glass still had blood in his body. Yet blood gurgled out of his torn throat with each labored breath.

"We need a couple volunteers to stay with the old man until he goes under," Major Henry said. "Then they can catch up. We got to get our fort built before winter."

"He cain't last long," someone said. "Jest look at what's left of a good man."

But no volunteers spoke up. They worried about other bears and the Arikaras.

"I'll pay money," Henry said. "You won't need to bury him. Just stay until he dies."

Finally, John Fitzgerald and young Jim Bridger agreed to stay. But old Hugh Glass was slow to die. Fitzgerald and Bridger fed him, washed his wounds, and brushed away the flies. They were afraid to shoot a gun or build a fire.

After five days they saw fresh Indian sign. Glass was feverish and nearly unconscious. They decided to leave him and rush on ahead. They did drag him to a spring.

They knew Major Henry would not believe that Glass had died unless they brought his rifle and other equipment. So they took the old man's rifle, powder-horn, bullet-pouch, axe, flint, and knife, and they sneaked away. When they caught up with the other trappers, they were praised for staying with the old man and not leaving him to die alone and defenseless.

Glass recovered consciousness and lay by the spring, eating berries and drinking water, until his fever left. He set out to the southeast, hoping to reach a trading fort before hostile Indians or wolves found him.

At first he could only crawl a few hundred yards a day. When he was crawling faster, he came upon wolves that had just killed a buffalo calf. He waited until they had satisfied their hunger; then he frightened them away and picked over the remains. He tore meat loose with his teeth and ate his fill and filled his shirt with more.

His strength now renewed, Glass was able to walk. Soon he reached the Missouri River. Friendly Sioux found him and took him to Fort Kiowa. He had traveled over two hundred miles.

Men at the fort looked at Glass' scarred and shrunken body and expected him to take the first boat downstream to recover his health in St. Louis.

"I got a score to settle, and I want my rifle back," the old man said.

He took the first boat upstream.

Again the Arikaras attacked; this time only Glass and one other passenger survived. When he reached the Mandan villages, he struck out overland — on foot in the snow — bound for the Bighorn.

The trappers at the fort thought a ghost had walked into their holiday celebrations when Glass arrived at the end of December. Glass let Bridger go because of his youth. He learned that Fitzgerald had gone back down the Missouri.

Glass left on February 29, continuing his journey of revenge. He walked into Fort Atkinson, downstream from Fort Kiowa, in May and learned that Fitzgerald had enlisted in the 6th Infantry there. Glass knew better than to kill a soldier, but he did recover his rifle.

Eight years later the Arikaras finally caught up with Hugh Glass in the Yellowstone country and killed him. The tough old man was out bear hunting at the time.

Suggested reading: John Myers Myers, *Pirate, Pawnee, and Mountain Man* (Boston: Little Brown, 1963).

HE SAVED HIS SCALP, BUT LOST HIS HAIR

James Clyman's first year in the mountains was memorable. The 31-year-old Virginian gave up a surveying job in Illinois to join the Ashley-Henry expedition in 1823.

Clyman escaped from the disastrous battle with the Arikaras by swimming across the Missouri River. As he climbed out of the water, unarmed and exhausted from nearly drowning, three Indians took up the chase. Clyman kept ahead of his pursuers for about an hour. Then he had what he called palpitations of the heart.

Fortunately Clyman saw a shallow, weed-covered depression when the Indians were temporarily out of sight. He dove in, hoping his frenzied breathing would quiet down before the Indians got there. The three pursuers sped past. When they were again out of sight, Clyman jumped up and ran into a ravine. He rested some more and then found his way back to the river. His party rescued him up as they floated downstream, in retreat from the battle.

After waiting for reinforcements to punish the Arikaras, the trappers continued west, traveling overland from a point near Fort Kiowa. When they reached the Cheyenne River near the Black Hills, a grizzly bear attacked Jedediah Smith, the captain of the Clyman party.

Blood was pouring from Smith's wounds when he asked Clyman to get a needle and thread and try to sew him up. Clyman had no experience, but he did his best.

"I got a pair of scissors and cut off his hair and then began my first job of dressing wounds," he wrote. "The bear had taken nearly all of his head in his capacious mouth, close to his left eye on one side and close to his right ear on the other, and laid the skull bare to near the crown of the head, leaving a white streak where his teeth passed. One of his ears was torn from his head out to the outer rim.

"After stitching all the other wounds according to the captain's directions, the ear being the last, I told him I could do nothing for the ear.

"'Oh, you must try to stitch up some way or other,' said he. Then I put in my needle, stitching it through and through and over and over, laying the lacerated parts together as nice as I could.

"This gave us a lesson on the character of the grizzly bear which we did not forget."

Clyman trapped that winter in the Wind River Mountains of present Wyoming. During one blizzard he saved William Sublette from freezing to death.

The next June Clyman got separated from his party while they were fighting Shoshoni horse thieves on the Sweetwater River. He stayed hidden from the Indians for eleven days. Once he walked backward through sandy ground to reach a rocky ledge, which he followed until he could cross running water. At times war parties of over twenty warriors almost found him.

After eleven days Clyman decided to head for the Missouri River. He followed the Sweetwater to the Platte, where he found an abandoned bull boat. He floated downstream among large herds of Buffalo.

He saw bands of wild horses. He made a halter out of buffalo hide, and he tried to crease a large black stallion that came to the river to drink. The horse fell, and Clyman ran up to put the halter on. Then he discovered that he had broken the animal's neck. The stallion lay at his feet, dead.

Clyman became so lonesome that when he saw a lodge trail crossing the river, he followed it, hoping to find company. He came to a village of Pawnee Indians.

Clyman had not had a haircut since leaving St. Louis a year and a half before. One of the Pawnees, impressed with Clyman's flowing mane, begged the white man for his hair. To keep the Indians friendly, Clyman let the man cut off his hair with a dull butcher knife.

Clyman eventually reached Fort Atkinson on the Missouri River. He had completed one of the longest solitary walks in the history of the Old West.

"I barely saved my scalp but lost my hair," he told the soldiers at the fort.

Within a few months, a year older and much wiser than when he had entered the mountains, Clyman headed west to trap another season.

James Clyman, *Journal of a Mountain Man* (Missoula: Mountain Press Publishing Co., 1984).

A LONESOME DEATH IN THE WILDERNESS

Hiram Scott volunteered for the Ashley-Henry Expedition in 1823.

Some of Scott's companions – Jedediah Smith, Thomas Fitzpatrick, William Sublette – became famous as mountain men. While Scott is seldom mentioned, he was to have one of the most prominent features of the western landscape, now a national monument, named for him. The honor came from the tragic circumstances of his death.

Soon after joining Ashley's expedition, Scott showed his leadership and ability. After the devastating attack by Arikaras, Colonel Henry Leavenworth marched up the Missouri with two hundred soldiers to punish the Indians. Ashley divided his men into two companies and turned them over to Leavenworth as volunteer soldiers.

"Hiram Scott and Jedediah Smith will captain the two new companies," Leavenworth ordered.

The volunteers received praise for their valor, but Leavenworth withdrew after brief skirmishes with nothing resolved.

Later, pressure from the Arikaras and the Blackfeet forced Ashley to abandon the Missouri River and move his operations southwest to the Rocky Mountains. The Rocky Mountain Fur Company grew and prospered, and Scott became a trusted lieutenant of Ashley.

The trappers began using the natural highway along the North Platte River to enter the mountains in the spring and to bring out their furs in the fall. A tall, sandstone bluff along the river in what is now southwestern Nebraska dominated the route. The sheer walls, twisted badlands, and towering crags looming eight hundred feet in the air were imposing sights on the high plains. The bluff would become a celebrated landmark on the Oregon Trail when emigrants began following the paths of the mountain men.

In fall 1828 the Rocky Mountain Fur Company trappers left their rendezvous at Great Salt Lake with about seventy-five mounted men and a mule train loaded with beaver pelts. William Sublette commanded the train, and Scott served as chief representative of the company owners.

Hostile Indians attacked as the trappers forded the North Platte at the Laramie fork. Several men were killed, and Scott was seriously wounded. The Indians also captured many mules and furs.

Scott's wounds prevented him from continuing on horseback. Both he and Sublette realized the importance of getting the rest of the furs out of hostile Indian country before the train was attacked again.

Sublette held the train while his men built a bull boat from brush-covered buffalo hides. He ordered two men to bring Scott down the river in the boat.

"I'll have help waiting for you at the tall bluff," Sublette said. "By traveling day and night in the boat, the three of you should catch up to the train there."

Scott, hovering between life and death, floated downstream with his two companions. They watched constantly for hostile Indians and wondered if they could really catch up with the train. But the river was low and navigation difficult. They kept running aground.

Before they could see the bluffs, the boat hit a snag, swamped, and overturned. All supplies, including the precious gunpowder, were lost. Scott's companions were barely able to recover their rifles and get their invalid leader to shore.

Without gunpowder the two caretakers knew that staying with their charge would mean starvation unless the Indians killed them first. The desperate predicament called for a quick decision.

They deserted Scott, probably telling themselves he was a goner anyway. They lied as they left, saying they would look for food and be right back.

The two men caught up with the pack train, reporting that Scott had been killed when the boat overturned. Not until the next spring, when Sublette led his men back up the Platte, did he learn that Scott had been abandoned while still alive. His hunters found Scott's skeleton just across the river from the tall bluff.

The names of the two men who cruelly abandoned their leader are unknown. We do know that Scott crawled about sixty miles in his desperate effort to catch up with the pack train. We do not know whether he was killed by Indians or starved to death. We can, however, imagine the terror and loneliness which certainly filled his thoughts as he crawled downstream and waited near the tall bluff for the help which never came.

The tall bluff was named Scotts' Bluff and now a national monument near Scottsbluff, Nebraska.

Suggested reading: Merrill J. Mattes, "Hiram Scott, Fur Trader," in *Nebraska History, 26(3)* (July-Sept., 1945).

PEGLEG

Thomas L. Smith had trapped in the Southwest for three years when he joined the Sylvestre Pratte expedition in Taos in fall 1827. The other trappers welcomed the 26-year-old Kentucky native; they knew he was tough. They traveled north to the headwaters of the North Platte and divided, Smith going on alone to the Big Sandy. When he realized that hostile Arapahoes were stalking him, he returned to the agreed rendezvous point.

As he approached his companions, a shot rang out from nearby bushes. Smith fell to the ground, his lower left leg shattered by an Indian bullet. Both leg bones, poking out from the wound, punched into the ground as Smith struggled back to recover his rifle.

A one-hour battle followed. The trappers killed nine Indians, including one in the bushes from where the shot came that hit Smith. During the battle, Smith tied a buckskin thong around his leg to control the bleeding.

When the battle ended, Smith begged his companions to cut his leg off. They stood in grim silence, none willing to cause Smith any more pain.

"Bring me your sharpest knife," Smith hollered to the cook. "I'll whack it off myself, if I have to."

He took the knife and worked slowly, his jaw clenched in pain. He trimmed away the torn muscles from the jagged fracture. When only the achilles tendon was left to hold the foot on and Smith was almost unconscious from pain, his friend, Milton Sublette, stepped forward.

"I'll finish up, Tom," Sublette said, quietly. "Man shouldn't have to do this to himself."

Sublette completed the amputation. He wanted to sear the stump with a hot iron, but Smith refused.

"Don't think I can handle any more, Milton," he said.

The other trappers wrapped the wound in a dirty shirt and made Smith as comfortable as possible. Everyone assumed that Smith would bleed to death.

"He's a tough old buffler, but surely he'll go under now," they said, nodding to each other.

"Don't leave me like they left old Glass," Smith pleaded.

"We'll stay, Tom."

Smith nodded grimly and asked for more whiskey.

The next morning, when the trappers came to look at Smith's corpse, he cursed them roundly. To everyone's surprise, the bleeding had stopped. They wondered if the freezing night air had coagulated the blood. In one more day Smith was strong enough to travel. Two of the men carried him in a litter. They traveled north and west to the Green River, where they stopped for the winter.

As the flesh sunk back from the stub, Smith found that a bone fragment projected which he could wiggle. Using a bullet mould for a forceps and with Sublette's help, Smith pulled the fragment out.

About forty lodges of Ute Indians spent the winter with the trappers. They used rituals of wailing and incantations to complete the healing of their friend's leg. Another bone fragment came loose. Again, using the bullet mould forceps, Smith pulled it out.

The other trappers made Smith a wooden leg from an oak branch. By spring he could walk on it. They began calling him Peg-leg.

Smith continued trapping until beaver became hard to find. Milton Sublette, the friend who had helped with the amputation, lost his leg in 1835, dying two years later.

Peg-leg, Jim Beckwourth, and Walkara, one of the Utes Smith had wintered with, took up horse stealing. In spring 1840 Peg-leg was one of the leaders in the largest horse-stealing raid in western history. They stole three thousand horses from Californio ranchos and missions. For the next ten years, Smith sold horses to Mormons and to emigrants going to Oregon and California.

The lure of gold brought Peg-leg to California to stay in 1850. He settled on a ranch near Sacramento. California pioneers remembered his help in providing horses in their journeys west. He had many friends, but his days of prosperity had ended. In 1852 the California State Senate petitioned the United States Congress to give financial aid to the old trapper. Governor John Bigler endorsed the resolution, but apparently Congress did not respond.

Peg-leg spent his final days in San Francisco. He became a familiar sight at the corner of Montgomery and Clay streets, shouting out Indian war whoops and asking friends for charity. An old friend got him admitted to the San Francisco County Hospital and kept him supplied with whiskey and tobacco. Peg-leg died there in October 1866, aged sixty-five.

Suggested reading: *San Francisco Bulletin,* October 26, 1886.

A FINE FUNERAL FOR A LONELY MAN

Sylvester Pattie was born on August 25, 1782. Another event on that day became an omen for much of his adult life. On the day of Sylvester's birth, his father helped bury forty-three men at Blue Lick, Kentucky, thirty miles north of the Pattie home. The settlers had been killed by Indians. Sylvester Pattie would spend much of his adult life fighting Indians.

Pattie grew up with explorer William Clark and with Jacob Fowler, who would later lead the first trapping party from Missouri to Santa Fe. Daniel Boone was a near neighbor.

When Pattie was twenty, he married Polly Hubbard. The next year, when Meriwether Lewis came down the Ohio to pick up William Clark for their great adventure, Sylvester paid little attention. He was busy farming, and his beloved Polly was pregnant.

Until 1811 Pattie resisted the call of his neighbors to move west. But then he sold his 145-acre farm and moved to Missouri with Polly, their five children, and the family slaves. He stopped temporarily in St. Charles, where he served in the militia in the war against the British. There he met William Ashley, Hiram Scott, Morgan Boone and others who would become famous in the fur trade.

At war's end Pattie moved on to the explored but as yet unsettled frontier in the northern Ozarks. There he built a sawmill and grist mill on Big Piney Creek at the mouth of another, unnamed, creek. That creek, named for its first settler, is still called Paddy Creek.

The mills drew new settlers to the area, and again Pattie prospered. Farmers needed construction lumber and mills to convert their crops into merchantable meal and flour. With an unlimited supply of pine timber, Pattie became wealthy. In 1820 he was the second largest taxpayer in Franklin County.

But Polly died about three years later, after giving birth to their ninth child. Sylvester's reaction was unusual on the frontier, where women often died during childbearing years. Overwhelmed by grief, he became silent and dejected.

Even after the usual period of mourning, when unmarried women began to smile hopefully, Pattie's depression never changed. The only thing that produced any interest were stories about trapping among Indians farther west. Finally, in spring 1824, he placed seven of the children with relatives in Kentucky (the baby had died with its mother), and with twenty-year-old John at his side, Sylvester headed west.

For the next four years, Pattie divided his time between trapping in New Mexico and operating copper mines for their Mexican owners. In 1828 he led a party of trappers down the Gila River. Some of the men returned to New Mexico. Pattie led the other seven, including James, on down the Colorado into Old Mexico.

Mexican authorities captured them and took them under guard to San Diego. Governor Jose Echeandia released two of the men and put the other six, including the two Patties, in jail.

Sylvester had almost died of thirst before he was captured. He stayed in poor health after the arrest. Mexican women in San Diego nursed him, treated him kindly, and persuaded him to become a catholic.

"I agree," Pattie said. "Where I'm going it will do no harm."

Don Jose Bernadino Pico, a sergeant in the Mexican Army, and Doña Victoria Dominguez de Estudillo served as Sylvester's sponsors at his baptism.

James Pattie was released to help Mexican authorities fight an epidemic. The sergeant's wife, Señora Pico, assured him that if his father died, she would see that he received a catholic burial.

Sylvester Pattie died on May 24, 1828, aged forty-five. His funeral was described as the grandest San Diego had ever seen.

A Franciscan priest led the procession. Four acolytes followed. Four Californios carried the coffin. The four trappers still in custody were released to attend. They and James, along with several crewmen from an American ship in the harbor, followed the coffin to the cemetery. Many San Diego residents brought up the rear.

After the catholic burial service ended, Señora Pico and several other women knelt around the grave to offer their prayers for the lonely foreign trapper whom they had taken to their hearts.

Suggested reading: Richard Batman, *James Pattie's West* (Norman: University of Oklahoma Press, 1984).

LIVING OFF THE LAND

Zenas Leonard's four-year trapping career, while short, included some of the most thrilling events in the history of the Old West. He fought in the Battle of Pierre's Hole, and was in Joseph Walker's overland expedition to California. He trapped for Captain Bonneville in the Yellowstone and Wind River Valleys. Leonard's most harrowing experience came during his first winter in the West when he learned, first hand, about living off the land.

Leonard, a 22-year-old farm boy, left St. Louis in April, 1831, as a clerk with Gantt and Blackwell, who hoped to compete with the Rocky Mountain Fur Company and the American Fur Company. Game was scarce as the trappers followed up the Kansas and Republican Rivers. They killed their last beef on June 21.

"Here we began to feel somewhat alarmed," Leonard wrote. "Starvation began to stare us in the face, and some of the company became refractory and were for turning back."

They kept on, however, hoping soon to find buffalo. They lived on small fish, which they caught in small creeks and rivers. Finally the captain ordered two of their best horses killed so the men would not starve. Then they headed north for the Platte to see if they could find buffalo. But with only an occasional wolf, wild cat, or antelope to eat, they stayed hungry. In the middle of July, at a place barren of wood and with nothing to eat if they did have a fire, they held a conference of desperation.

"Despondency and horror were depicted in the countenance of every man," Leonard wrote. "The enquiry, 'what shall we do?' was passing from every lip."

Again the company decided to push ahead. They reached the Platte the next night. Two elk killed there kept them alive until they found buffalo. Game was abundant all along the river. They stopped at the Laramie River in late August to reconnoiter for fall trapping.

The fifty to sixty men in the company divided into three parties for the season. Leonard's party would go up the Laramie under Captain A. K. Stephens. The three parties planned to re-unite at the mouth of the Laramie in late December and spend the rest of the winter there.

Stephens' party trapped until October 25, when they decided to head back downstream toward the rendezvous point. Five days later, finding the snow too deep for travel, they decided to winter in a wide valley and return to the river mouth in spring.

They built cabins and killed buffalo. They dried the meat to ensure a supply of food if the buffalo should leave the valley. By December 1, they were feeding cottonwood bark to their horses.

They couldn't find enough bark, and the horses began dying. By early January only two mules remained. They still had dried meat to eat, but the men worried about getting out of the snow-filled valley with no horses to carry their fur.

On January 14, leaving four men behind to care for the two mules and the fur, the rest set out for Santa Fe, eight hundred miles to the south. Each man carried nine beaver pelts, which they planned to trade for horses.

As they moved south they climbed higher and higher. Finally the slopes were too steep and the snow too deep to continue. They were out of food, and they feared starvation if they turned back to the wide valley they had left. They had started to eat their beaver skins. They made snowshoes out of the skin overcoats some of the men wore and out of the deerskin lining in some of their pants.

Leonard said they were in a "desolate wilderness, uninhabited by even the hardy savage or wild beast, surrounded on either side by huge mountains of snow, without one mouthful to eat, save a few beaver skins, our eyes almost destroyed by the piercing wind, and our bodies at times almost buried by the flakes of snow which were driven before it."

On February 4 someone saw two animals feeding in the brush. Leonard and a Mr. Hockaday, the strongest men left, were chosen to approach and kill the animals, whatever they were.

The two men crawled on hands and knees to within fifty yards of the animals, which they recognized as buffalo. Hockaday was too weak to hold his rifle up.

"You shoot, Zenas," he said. "I cain't hold her steady."

Leonard's rifle misfired. The buffalo continued to browse until he could fire again. This time he broke the back of one of the animals.

For nine days the men had eaten nothing but beaver pelts. They feasted on the buffalo for four days and then moved on, finding more game.

After a battle with Indians, the trappers gave up on going to Santa Fe. They turned back north and reached the mouth of the Laramie River on May 20, five months late. They sold their furs to the Rocky Mountain Fur Company, and went their separate ways.

Suggested reading: John C. Ewers (ed.) *Adventures of Zenas Leonard, Fur Trader* (Norman: Univ. of Okla. Press, 1959).

A WILD CHASE

Thomas Fitzpatrick best represents the mountain men who roamed the Rockies for thirty years, trapping beaver, fighting Indians, and guiding explorers and settlers. He immigrated from Ireland in 1816, when he was seventeen. We know little about his youth except that he came from a good Catholic family and was well educated. He went up the Missouri with Ashley's second expedition and fought in the great battle against the Arikaras. He led trapper bands and became head of the Rocky Mountain Fur Company. He was in the small party that discovered South Pass, the gateway to Oregon. He guided the first emigrant train over the Oregon Trail. Before that he guided Fremont across the Sierras and Father De Smet to the Flathead Indians. He was the first Indian agent appointed for the plains tribes, a position he held until he died.

Fitzpatrick had two nicknames. Broken Hand came from a disfiguring injury. White Hair resulted from a wild chase by Indians in 1832.

In that year Fitzpatrick was traveling with the supply train to the company rendezvous at Pierre's Hole, when he stopped at the mouth of the Laramie River to buy furs from another trapping party. He cached the furs and hurried on west, alone, to tell his partners and their trappers that the supply train was approaching.

Fitzpatrick traveled with two fast horses, which he rode alternately. He thought his mounts' speed would keep him safe from hostile Indians.

He had no trouble until he crossed South Pass and started down the western slope. Then he and a large band of Atsinas saw each other at the same time. That tribe hated whites and they tried to kill them whenever they found one or a few out by themselves.

Fitzpatrick knew he was in a race for his life. He spun his horse around and galloped off. In turning so quickly, his led horse pulled away and escaped. Fitzpatrick felt his mount's straining muscles and heaving chest as it struggled up a steep slope. The gallant animal flagged and slowed to a walk, in spite of the rider's whip flailing against its ribs.

The Indian horses also gave out, but the warriors, now yelling in glee, jumped to the ground and continued the chase on foot. Seeing the Indians gaining, Fitzpatrick vaulted from his horse and scrambled up the rough slope, blood-thirsty cries ringing behind him.

Fitzpatrick gained some on his Indian pursuers. He found a

hole in the rocks, slipped in, and quickly closed the mouth with sticks and leaves. Triumphant yells told him that his horse had been caught. Then scurrying footsteps past his hiding place made his heart sound, to him, like a roaring volcano.

But the footsteps receded in the distance, and Fitzpatrick lay for hours in a despairing silence until darkness came. He crawled out, looked over the country, and started off in what seemed the safest direction. When he realized that he had reached the edge of the Indian camp, he breathed a prayer of thanks that no one was on guard. He was able to get back to his hiding place safely.

Early the next morning, he heard Indian voices, and he knew they had resumed their search. When the voices could no longer be heard, he crept to the mouth of the hole and saw Indians running races with his horse.

Fitzpatrick remained in his hiding place all the second day. After dark he slipped out, climbed down the mountain, and followed a creek that flowed away from the Indian camp. He hid in brush all day and continued his travel the third night.

When daylight came, Fitzpatrick kept traveling. He thought he was outside the range of the Indians' pursuit. He found some berries and roots, his first food during the three-day ordeal. He had kept his rifle, but he dared not shoot at game, afraid the Indians would hear his shot.

When Fitzpatrick came to a stream, he built a crude raft and pushed it into the water. The raft broke up on a rock, and he lost his rifle in the swift current. Now he had no weapon but his knife.

He struggled on, weak and staggering, toward the rendezvous point at Pierre's Hole. One night, while he dug for roots in a swamp, a pack of wolves found him. He escaped up a tree, where he stayed until daybreak.

He found a buffalo, killed and partly eaten by wolves. He scraped what he could from the bones. But berries and roots became harder to find. He got weaker and could no longer walk. Finally, Fitzpatrick gave up hope and waited for death.

Two trappers from the rendezvous found their leader. They could hardly recognize him. His body was a skeleton, and his eyes seemed sunken, deep and dark, into a shrunken face. His hair had turned permanently white.

Suggested reading: LeRoy R. Hafen, *Broken Hand* (Lincoln: University of Nebraska Press, 1973).

THE BATTLE OF PIERRE'S HOLE

The 1832 rendezvous was big, colorful and exciting. It ended with one of the largest battles between Indians and civilians in North American history.

The rendezvous, held in a beautiful valley just west of Teton Pass in present Idaho, drew trappers from the American Fur Company, the Hudson's Bay Company, the Rocky Mountain Fur Company, and several smaller, independent companies. In all, about a thousand persons, including friendly Nez Perce and Flathead Indians, plus almost three thousand horses and mules, gathered in the valley.

After two weeks of shooting contests, horse racing, singing, bragging, and wrestling, the rendezvous degenerated into a drunken brawl. Shoshoni maidens, ready to bestow favors for pretty beads and blankets, added to the explosive mix. One trapper poured a pot of whiskey over another, repeating what he thought was a baptismal ceremony. Another man threw a match. Fortunately, some fairly sober bystanders beat out the human bonfire with packsaddles. The poor victim almost died and never fully recovered.

The rendezvous broke up on July 17, when Milton Sublette and Joe Meek moved their men out. Nathaniel Wyeth's New Englanders and a free company under Alexander Sinclair traveled with them, making a group of about sixty, many fairly new to trapping. They camped the first night about eight miles from the rendezvous.

The next morning a large band of Atsinas descended into the valley from a high pass. Two of Sublette's Indians, a half blood Iroquois and a Flathead, rode forward to meet the Atsinas.

The approaching Indians, knowing they had been seen, rode forward at a gallop and brandished their weapons. The principal chief of the Atsinas, riding in front, held out a peace pipe. The trappers and their Indians were sure, based on experience, that the chief was stalling until his warriors were in position to attack. The Iroquois took the pipe while the Flathead shot the chief. Sublette's Indians galloped back to the trappers, and the Atsinas moved into a swamp, thickly overgrown with cottonwoods, willows and vines.

Shooting on both sides was sporadic at first. A messenger rode back to the rendezvous site for reinforcements. Sublette's brother, William, arrived with a large group. Other groups followed, and the astonished Atsinas saw what they thought would be a short battle to kill hated whites turn into one of desperate defense.

When William Sublette rode up, he and his friend, Robert Campbell, along with Sinclair, led the way into the thick, tangled growth. The Atsinas had built a rude fort of logs and buffalo robes, and had sent their women and children back into the mountains. Dislodging the Indians would obviously be difficult.

The three leaders repeated their oral wills as they moved forward. Sinclair was the first to fall. Before he died he asked Campbell to see that his body was taken to his brother, Prewitt Sinclair, also present at the rendezvous.

Just after William Sublette dropped an Indian, he took a bullet in the shoulder. Campbell and Joe Meek carried him out of the thicket. Sublette's trappers worked in toward one side of the fort and Wyeth's Nez Perces toward the other. While the cross fire was deadly for the entrenched Atsinas, it also struck several of the trappers' own men.

As more and more arrived from the rendezvous, the Atsina guns finally became silent. But the trappers were unable to dislodge the Indians, now out of ammunition but still waiting with bows and arrows for the slightest enemy movement.

Nez Perces and Flatheads gathered dry sticks to set fire to the breastworks. But an old Atsina chief shouted from his hidden lair: "Four hundred lodges of our people are close by. They will avenge our deaths, ten for one."

The trappers misunderstood and thought the chief had announced a present attack back at the rendezvous. Leaving a small force to watch the Indian fort, the rest of the trappers galloped back to rescue the main camp. When they learned that the alarm was false, it was too late to return to the fort.

After a cautious advance the next morning, the trappers found the fort abandoned. Ten dead Atsinas lay inside the fort and others outside. The trappers recovered thirty horses that had been stolen weeks before from William Sublette's group as he approached the rendezvous. In addition to Sinclair, five other trappers and eight friendly Indians had been killed.

The trappers found one live person, a despondent old woman. She leaned against a tree, a corpse at her feet.

"Kill me, kill me, oh white man, kill me," she pleaded. "You got my man. Now kill me."

The trappers refused but one of their friendly Indians obliged, and one more Atsina fell at the Battle of Pierre's Hole.

Suggested reading: Frances F. Victor, *The River of the West* (Missoula: Mountain Press Publ. Co., 1983).

A WILD RIDE IN A PLUM THICKET

Plums were thick along Pryor's Fork of the Yellowstone that fall of 1836. As Joe Meek and David Crow searched for a place to set traps, they wondered if Blackfeet might be around picking fruit. They didn't see anything suspicious, so Meek set two traps by an old beaver dam among the plum trees. Then they rode downstream where Crow set his traps.

After a wild ride the next day to reach the camp of other trappers, Meek explained what had happened.

"After we got our traps set yesterday morning, we cruised around and ate plums awhile," he told Jim Bridger. "They was the best plums I ever saw. The trees are loaded and breaking down to the ground. They're as large as pheasant eggs and sweet as sugar. They almost melt in your mouth. No wonder them rascally savages like that place so well."

"What happened?" Bridger asked.

"Well, after we had our fill of plums, me and Dave took down the creek and stayed all night on a little branch in the hills. Then this morning we rode back up to check on our traps. A couple of Dave's traps had been sprung, but he didn't have nothing. We rode on up to mine and I was riding five or six steps ahead when I saw a buffalo running and a bear come out of the willows like he had been disturbed. I told Crow I didn't like the looks of it and I didn't want to go into the thicket."

"Red devils in there?" asked one of the trappers who had gathered around.

"Crow laughed and called me a coward if I wouldn't go in to my traps. Then I got mad and started in. When I got opposite the first trap, I heard a rustling in the bushes. I looked around, and pop! pop! pop! went them Injun guns. They covered me with smoke so close I could see the wads coming out of their muzzles."

"They hit you?" asked a trapper.

"I wheeled and a ball struck Two Shebit here in the neck." He patted the dried blood on his white horse. "We pitched heels over head, but Two Shebit come up a'runnin and I still on his back. The savages was grabbin' at me, but I raised a fog for half a mile until I overtook Dave.

"Being mounted, we had the advantage, but I had to stop after a mile and breathe my horse. When the Injuns come up, we killed the two in front. We rode another mile and killed two more in front. Them Blackfeet can run almost as good as a trapper. We did that once more, and I guess they figured they'd had enough. Seven dead savages — I had killed one in the thicket — and they still didn't have a white scalp. I reckon they had run about all they had wanted to, anyway.

Meek and Crow then learned from the other trappers that several war parties of Blackfeet had been seen scouting around the country.

"We run into another party of Blackfeet just a few days ago," Meek said. "We were crossing the pass from the Gallatin into the Yellowstone basin. That's how come we're down this way. They give us a scare, but we burned the wind and got away. I told Crow maybe we're getting too old for this."

Two days after Meek and Crow's second wild ride, sixty Blackfeet killed a French trapper named Bordeaux on a nearby creek.

When Bridger's party reached the mouth of Pryor's Fork, they rode upstream to get some plums of their own. We don't know if Meek and Crow were still with them.

Crow was killed the following year in a freak accident at Fort Laramie. He was in a group of Bridger's men who had stopped at the fort to celebrate the Christmas holidays. The men had stuffed a cannon so it would make a loud report. The fort gunner refused to fire the weapon.

"It'll blow up, sure," he warned.

David Crow took an iron rod from a fire and touched off the fuse. The cannon exploded into a hundred pieces. One of them broke Crow's leg. Someone at the fort dressed the wound too tightly, mortification set in, and Crow died.

When Meek's trapping days ended, he settled in the Oregon country, becoming its first sheriff. He also served in the Oregon Provisional Legislature. He carried the news east of the Whitman Massacre and the plea of Oregon residents for organization under the laws of the United States. On his way he stopped at the ruins of the Whitman Mission to bury his daughter, Helen Mar Meek, who had been killed there. She was the child of the second of his three Indian wives. Meek also had to stop at Fort Bridger and tell his old friend that his daughter, Mary Ann Bridger, had also been killed. The two trappers had left their daughters with Narcissa Whitman to be properly educated.

Meek brought back news that Oregon would be part of the United States and that he would be the terrritory's first United States Marshal. The fact that President Polk had married Meek's cousin probably helped.

Suggested reading: Stanley Vestal, *Joe Meek, The Merry Mountain Man* (Caldwell The Caxton Printers, 1952).

JOE MEEK

Oregon Historical Society, Neg. No. OrHi 3474

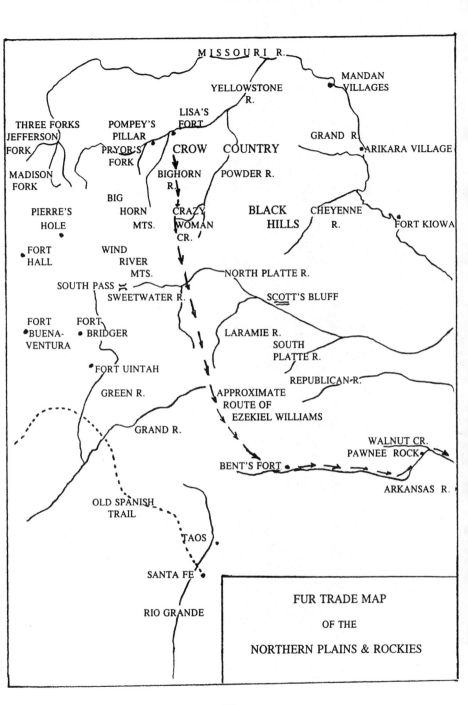

FUR TRADE MAP

OF THE

NORTHERN PLAINS & ROCKIES

CRAZY WOMAN CREEK

A beautiful creek running through ancient Crow hunting grounds in present Wyoming was originally called Beard Creek after the long, bearded grass in its valley. Early in the nineteenth century a half-blood trader came to the valley and built a cabin and storehouse for his large supply of beads and ribbons. The cottonwood-shaded creek flowed through a fertile land. Prairie chickens, grouse, and ducks flew above the tall grass. Deer, elk, antelope, and buffalo grazed on the rolling plains. The trader soon had all the robes and furs the Crows had for trade. He packed them out on his horses, promising to return.

The trader had a fair-skinned woman with him when he came back, this time with wagons. The woman kept her long hair wrapped and covered with a bonnet. Her long dresses made the Indians wonder if she was ashamed of her legs and feet.

The trader unloaded his wagons and opened his store. He had ribbons for the women and brass rings for the men. All the people loved him. They had never seen such a generous and wealthy man.

One day the trader took the chief to the back of his store. He drew a dark liquid out of a barrel and told the chief to drink. Soon the chief felt so jolly he wanted more.

"You can have all you want if you never tell your people where you got the happy water," the trader said.

The chief promised. After drinking more he began to sing and dance. Then he returned to his lodge and fell into a long sleep.

The next day the chief told the trader about his many pleasant dreams of slaying enemies.

"I want more of the dark, magic water," he said.

The people began to wonder if the trader had bewitched the chief. Before, he had been quiet and dignified; now he sang, danced, and publicly hugged women. The people thought their leader crazy, and they grumbled and complained about the trader. A council was called; it decided the trader had to leave or be put to death.

A warrior friend of the trader brought him the news. The trader took his friend to the back of the store.

"If you won't tell anyone, you can know the truth about your chief," he said.

The warrior agreed. Soon the warrior began singing and dancing. Young men gathered around, wondering about the warrior's strange behavior and asking him what had happened.

But the warrior fell asleep, and the people continued to wonder and talk.

Every day the chief and the warrior got drunk. The people were baffled.

"I watched through a hole in the wall," one of them said. "The trader fed a dark drink to our chief and the brave. They smacked their lips and asked for more."

The council summoned the trader before them to explain.

"Yes, I have black medicine water," he said. "All who drink it have pleasant dreams of killing enemies."

Other men came to the cabin to drink of the dark, magic water. Soon they sang and danced, and many slept a long time.

After a few weeks the trader said he could give them no more unless they paid. At first the price was one robe for one sleep. After a time the trader said he had only a little left for his own use. But the Indians begged, and he gave them more, now charging many robes for a sleep. After all the robes were in the trader's storeroom, the Indians traded horses. Then they offered their women, but the medicine water barrels were empty. The trader packed his robes and furs, saying he would return in the spring.

"You may not go," the Indians said. "You have hidden the medicine water and will trade it to our Sioux enemies."

They searched the trader's packs, but found nothing. They chased him into his cabin and killed him in front of his pale-skinned woman. They ripped off his scalp and stamped his body with their feet. The woman tried to run, but they knocked her down.

The warriors burned the trader's cabin and store and took back all their robes, furs and horses. The Indian women sewed up the wounds of the white woman and fed her. But when she was well, she had become crazy, believing that any warrior who approached would kill her. She ran away and hid in the bluffs along the creek. Indian women took food to her and asked her to return, but she refused. Whenever the warriors came out, she hid in terror.

When the village returned to the creek after their winter camp, the Indians could no longer find the white woman. No one knew whether she starved or was killed by bears. From then on the Indians called the creek, Crazy Woman Creek, still its present name.

Suggested reading: James S. Brisbin, *Belden, the White Chief* (Athens: Ohio University Press, 1974).

47

SCALP HUNTER

Jim Kirker immigrated to the United States from Ireland in 1810 when he was seventeen. He became a legal pirate, serving on a U. S. privateer in the War of 1812. Captured by the British, he was returned in a prisoner exchange before his captors discovered his nationality. They would have executed him for treason had they known.

After the war Kirker returned to his old job in a New York City grocery store. But selling groceries was dull, so Kirker headed west for adventure.

In 1821 he fought Comanches on the Santa Fe Trail. The next year he fought Arikaras on the Missouri River with the first Ashley-Henry expedition.

In 1825 Kirker returned to the Southwest, trapping beaver in New Mexico and Chihuahua. For the next several years, he trapped beaver in the winter and guided ore trains in the summer, all in Apache country.

In 1835 Kirker got a Mexican license to trade with Apaches. He lived with the tribe, and the Apaches made him a war chief. But suspicions that he was helping Apaches steal horses lost him his license. With a price on his head, Kirker went to Bent's fort to hide out.

The Mexican governor was killed, and Kirker was invited back by the new governor. A few months before, Kirker led a raid on an Apache village, killing fifty-five Indians and capturing four hundred horses. His fame as an Indian fighter spread across northern Mexico.

The Apaches had learned to "harvest" Mexican settlements. When they raided they never took quite all the food and material possessions. They always left enough that the surviving residents, instead of abandoning their homes, stayed and planted again.

The Mexican government hired Kirker to kill Apaches.

"We'll pay you one hundred dollars for a warrior's scalp, fifty for a woman's, and twenty-five for a child's," the government said.

After recruiting a motley army of a hundred or so mountain men and friendly Shawnee and Delaware Indians, Kirker became a professional Indian killer.

The high point of Kirker's scalp hunting came in 1843. Apaches had attacked a supply train of eighty mules outside Chihuahua City. They captured the train, killing all but one of the crew. The Mexican government offered Kirker all the mules and half of any merchandise recovered. Adding the bounty for Apache scalps, he stood to get rich. He led his men to the attack.

48

They caught up with the captured train and found the Indians passed out from stolen liquor. Kirker and his men slipped into the camp and cut every throat and ripped off every scalp. They recovered forty-three of the mules before the others got away. Then they turned to the liquor supply themselves. The triumphant army got as drunk as the Indians they had just killed. When they sobered up, Kirker told his men about a village of a thousand Apaches, three days away. For a fortune in scalps, the men needed no urging.

They reached the village as a party of warriors was returning from the direction of Sonora. The Apaches carried jugs of liquor on their shoulders. Fresh scalps dangled from their belts. Kirker and his men waited for the stolen liquor to make their prey helpless.

But someone fired too soon, and the Apache camp was alarmed. Under their chief, Cochise, most of the Apaches escaped. Kirker's Indians were downhearted. They had hoped to take enough scalps that they could retire to their eastern homelands.

The Mexicans met Kirker's army with a brass band when it returned with over a hundred wet scalps and eighteen captured Apache women. When the Chihuahua governor grumbled at counting the "walking scalps," for bounty purposes, Kirker's men offered to remove the women's scalps at once. The governor hastily agreed to give them full credit.

Unfortunately the governor's treasury had insufficient funds to pay what Kirker had coming.

"Pay up or we fight you," Kirker's men shouted.

The governor mobilized his troops to protect the palace. Kirker's irate Indians marched straight through the Mexicans and told the worried governor what they thought of his perfidy.

When Kirker's army rode north, leaving an empty treasury behind, the army's Indians said their only regret was that they had not taken the governor's scalp also.

The Mexican Government, facing a fight with the United States, offered Kirker the rank of full colonel. He declined and became a scout for Alexander Doniphan, who commanded a brigade of Missouri volunteers. Kirker was decorated for gallantry at the Battle of Sacramento on February 28, 1847.

Kirker later ranched in Contra Costa County, California, where a pass and a road have been named for him.

Suggested reading: William C. McGaw, *Savage Scene* (New York: Hastings House, 1972).

OLD MAN OF THE MOUNTAINS

Isaac Slover liked bear hunting better than tending his Arkansas farm. The Pennsylvania native had gradually worked his way west, moving from one hunting area to the next. In 1821, when he was forty-one, he jumped at the chance to go further west and trap. His party was the first to go down the Santa Fe Trail.

Companions described Slover as quiet, peaceable and reserved. They appreciated his experience and hunting skill. But he accepted no advice about his hunting methods and heeded no warnings about their danger.

Slover often left camp alone to hunt for weeks at a time. He always returned with happy stories of the bears he had killed. His favorite prey were grizzlies. He called them Cabibs. Many times, in returning to camp with fresh beaver pelts, he would call out with a wide grin, "Got me a couple more Cabibs!"

Slover's experience and age soon made him the leading hunter in the Southwest. Within a few years, Jim Bridger, Thomas Fitzpatrick, Kit Carson, William Bent, and the Sublette brothers all called him friend.

In 1828 Slover joined a trapping party led by Sylvester Pattie and his son, James. Slover, forty-seven, was the oldest of the group and the best hunter. After trapping down the Gila River, the party split up. Slover stayed with the Patties and four other men to trap on down the Colorado River into Old Mexico.

After unspeakable hardships from thirst and heat during which one member tried suicide and Slover and Sylvester Pattie had laid down to die, the party was rescued by Christian Indians. However Mexican authorities arrested them as illegal immigrants and took them under guard to San Diego. Slover and his friend, William Pope, were released together and allowed to travel to Sonora, perhaps for repatriation.

When they reached New Mexico, the two trappers married Spanish women. Friends of Slover's wife affectionately called her Doña Barbarita.

In 1837 Slover and Pope and their families returned to California with a colonizing expedition. Pope stopped near Los Angeles for a time and then moved north to settle in present Napa County. He accidentally cut his leg with an axe and bled to death. His valley and the creek running through it were named in his honor.

Slover's colony, in which he was the only Anglo-American, settled near present San Bernardino. The colony formed two new settlements on the Santa Ana River. Slover became the principal leader in one of them, Agua Mansa. His fellow settlers respected his wise counsel and experience.

Slover and his wife loved their little home at the foot of a

mountain near present Colton. Doña Barbarita made the lightest tortillas in the community. Visitors to the village always stopped at the Slover cabin to enjoy the hospitality of Isaac and his wife.

From his window Isaac could see the San Bernardino Mountains, still filled with game. As in his younger days, he still disappeared into the woods for days at a time. When he reached sixty-five, Slover's friends tried to talk him out of so much hunting. It was like talking to a deaf man. His greatest joy still came from hunting grizzlies.

On October 13, 1854, Isaac Slover, now seventy-five, was hunting on the north slope of Mount San Antonio, near Cajon Pass. He saw a grizzly and prepared to shoot. The rifle roared, the bear dropped, and the old man's face broke into a familiar grin. The huge bear crawled into heavy underbrush. Slover was surprised at the size of the animal.

The white-haired old man approached the brush carefully. This Cabib might need a sight more killing before he's through, he thought.

The wounded bear roared out of the brush, screaming in fury, blood spurting from its body. With no time to aim and not trusting a quick, slap shot from the hip, Isaac Slover dropped his rifle and grabbed his knife.

He smelled the bear's fetid breath and felt the warm blood spray as he drew his arm back. He plunged the knife deeply into the bear's neck, as he twisted his own body to one side. He heard the animal's teeth clack together in a frenzied miss. But sharp claws dug bone deep into his shoulder, and the old man knew he had been hurt bad.

When neighbors came up the mountain, they found the huge bear lying in the gore from its rifle and knife wounds. But nearby lay the torn and mangled body of their gray-haired friend, who had killed his last grizzly.

The neighbors carried Slover down to his home, where he died the next day. They named the mountain behind his cabin, Slover Mountain.

Suggested reading: John Brown and John Boyd, *History of San Bernardino and Riverside Counties* (Chicago, 1922).

HORSE STEALING, MOUNTAIN MAN STYLE

Horses brought to California by early Spaniards multiplied so fast they became a nuisance. Some town alcaldes ordered wild horses rounded up and killed to protect gentled horses and their pasturage. With an inexhaustible supply of wild horses available for breaking, gentled horses weren't worth much.

When the first pack train from Santa Fe reached Los Angeles in 1830, the New Mexico traders exchanged their woolen goods for California horses and mules. A ten dollar horse or mule in California brought five times that much in the Rockies.

About the same time, trapper Pegleg Smith reached California to trade furs. Mexican authorities ordered him out of the country. Perhaps they were not interested in furs; perhaps they thought Pegleg should first buy a trader's license. At any rate a spiteful Pegleg and his party stole about four hundred California horses as they rode away.

Other mountain men soon learned that they could supplement their trapping income by stealing California horses. By 1833 Alcalde Carrillo of Los Angeles wrote Governor Figueroa that at least one thousand mules had been stolen by men from New Mexico.

"If the matter is not checked soon, everything in the country will be taken away by the robbers," Carrillo complained.

Californians began calling the Old Spanish Trail to New Mexico the Thieves' Trail. Governor Figueroa immediately ordered all trappers out of California. The thieves were using the Tulares Valley, north of Los Angeles, as a place to gather the stolen horses before starting across the desert. The governor decreed that all horses in the Tulares Valley and the Mohave Desert were to be considered stolen and their possessors immediately arrested. Military commands at San Diego, Santa Barbara, and Monterey scoured the country for horse thieves.

The stealing continued. The most spectacular raid by mountain men came in 1840, after the beaver trade began its decline. The attacks started in mid May at Mission San Gabriel. Follow-up attacks on ranchos from San Bernardino in the east to Mission San Juan Capistrano in the south appeared to be well coordinated. Separate bands of thieves struck as far north as Mission San Luis Obispo, midway between Los Angeles and San Francisco. That mission lost twelve hundred horses in one night's raid. Mexican authorities released prisoners throughout the southern part of California to beef up their pursuing posses.

By the time three thousand stolen horses had been

accumulated, the thieves had trouble keeping their herd together. They divided their forces. Some drove the captive animals up the Old Spanish Trail. Others stayed behind, waiting to ambush pursuers.

An advance party of Mexican Cavalry caught up with the thieves at Rabbit Springs in the Mohave Desert. But when the Mexicans dismounted to rest and plan their attack, the Americans captured their horses and rode on. The cursing cavalrymen went back down the trail on foot.

Another pursuing party of Californians caught up with the thieves, who abandoned their horses and fled. The Californians said that half the stolen horses had already died from thirst and exhaustion. Reports of horse skeletons along the Old Spanish Trail for years to follow showed that many of the stolen horses did perish.

Different men have been accused of leading the mammoth raid. Pegleg Smith, Old Bill Williams, and Philip Thompson are most often mentioned. Horace Bell, early California Ranger, said Smith led fifteen white men and 150 Indians on the raid. Walkara, the notorious Ute chieftain, provided Indians for Smith. Apparently it was Smith's group that raided at Mission San Luis Obispo.

Lieutenant George D. Brewerton said Williams was in overall charge of the raid, leading thirty men. He mentioned the capture of the cavalry horses at Rabbit Springs. Brewerton, traveling over the Old Spanish Trail with Kit Carson in 1848, reported seeing many horse skeletons.

Rufus Sage, who met Philip Thompson driving horses to the Missouri River in 1841, said Thompson led twenty-two men on the raid the year before, capturing between two thousand and three thousand horses. Sage also mentioned the capture of the Mexican Cavalry horses.

Probably all three mountain men were with the marauders. It is doubtful that any one man was in overall command. But the raid they led in 1840 was certainly the largest horse-stealing operation in the West.

Suggested reading: Leroy R. Hafen, *Old Spanish Trail* (Glendale: Arthur H. Clark Co., 1954).

A SHORT, SPECTACULAR CAREER

Miles Goodyear's career in the West was short but spectacular. Born in Connecticut, he was orphaned at four and bound out to Squire Peck, a farmer, who agreed to feed him for what work he could do.

One year after his contract expired, seventeen-year-old Miles headed west and never looked back. Two years later, in 1836, the Whitman-Spalding missionary party saw him trudging along the trail. He carried a rusty gun and an empty powder horn, and he wore buckskin pants, half a shirt and one moccasin.

The missionaries were traveling with the supply train for the fur trappers' rendezvous, and they became the first party to cross the country with wagons. They hired Miles to help.

The young man was thrilled to meet such trappers as Thomas Fitzpatrick, Black Harris, and Milton Sublette, who were traveling with the train. But much backbreaking work fell on Miles. Tired of pushing a wagon, he left the Whitman party at Fort Hall and spent the winter trapping on Blackfoot Creek, about forty miles away.

For the next five years, Miles hunted, trapped and traded out of Fort Hall. He married the daughter of a Ute chief, and she bore him two children.

Miles was in Fort Uintah in 1842 when Marcus Whitman came through on his famous horseback ride to the United States. Miles wrote his family for the first time in eight years, sending the letter with Whitman.

Miles was in Fort Bridger in 1843. He earned a reputation for courage and daring in leading the pursuit after Cheyenne and Arapaho Indians, who had raided the fort's horse herd. Later that summer William Drummond Stewart invited Miles to join his legendary pleasure excursion in the Green River Valley.

Miles had no intention of ever returning to the East. He wanted to build a home in some beautiful valley where he would be free and independent from the rest of the world. He built his home in the Cache Valley where Ogden, Utah, now stands. He called it Fort Buenaventura. It was the first private home in the Great Basin. Miles planted gardens and kept livestock for trade with Indians and emigrants.

Miles left his family at the fort, and led a pack train carrying dressed deer hides and elk skins to Los Angeles in January, 1847. He sold his merchandise to John C. Fremont's rag-tag battalion, then fighting in the California rebellion. The soldiers needed the skins for clothing.

Miles used the money to buy several hundred horses. He

drove them to Sutter's Fort, and then across the Nevada-Utah basin to Fort Bridger, where he sold the horses to emigrants on the Oregon-California trail. When Miles crossed the Sierras, he became one of the first to see the remains of the Donner-Reed winter camp.

Leaders of the Mormon migration in 1847 had heard of the man who had a home in the Great Salt Lake Valley. They were glad to know that he could raise gardens and crops. They were even gladder when he agreed to sell his fort to them. By this time Miles' brother Andrew had come west to join him.

Miles returned to California, bought 230 horses from Californio Ranchos and drove them all the way to St. Joseph, Missouri. At the end of this, one of the longest stock drives in United States history, Miles hoped to sell the horses to west-bound emigrants.

While he was spending the 1848-1849 winter at St. Joseph with his horse herd, Miles heard of the gold discovery in California. He bought more horses and mules in Missouri, drove the larger herd back to California and sold them to prospectors there. Then he and Andrew started prospecting on the Yuba River.

Miles struck it rich at a place still called Goodyear's Bar. He had fallen in love with the country around Benicia, California, and hoped someday to build his dream home there. But in November, 1849, he caught a fever and died, aged thirty-two.

Miles Goodyear had little education, but he loved writing poetry. His letter back home, which had brought Andrew out West, ended:

> My home's amid the mountains wild,
> The land I fancied from a child,
> To climb the cliff or tread the vale,
> Where care nor trouble ne'er prevail,
> To hunt the roe, the stag, the deer,
> Or breathe the mountin air so clear,
> Or chase the buffalo o'er the plain,
> For here I am and here I remain.

Andrew honored Miles' last wish and buried him in Benicia.

Miles Goodyear's career in the West was short. But it would be hard to cram more interesting people or events into thirteen years.

Suggested reading: Charles Kelly and Maurice Howe, *Miles Goodyear: First Citizen of Utah* (Salt Lake City: Western Printing Co., 1937).

LOYALTY BEYOND THE CUSTOM OF THE COUNTRY

Daniel W. Harmon of Vermont became a fur trader in 1800 when he was twenty-two. His strict New England puritanism insulated him from the celebrated charms of the Ojibway women. After being away from civilization for eighteen months, Harmon was offered the pretty daughter of a Cree chief. Knowing the advantage his employer, the Northwest Company, would gain in access to furs from the chief's band, Harmon thought long and hard before declining.

"Happily for me," he wrote, "I escaped the snare."

But three more years in the wilderness took their toll on Harmon's puritanism. On the headwaters of the Saskatchewan, he was offered another girl, aged about fourteen. After "mature consideration," he accepted.

"I have finally concluded to accept her," he wrote in his journal, "as it is customary for all gentlemen who remain for any length of time in this part of the world to have a female companion with whom they can pass their time more socially and agreeably than to live a lonely life, as they must do if single."

He named his bride Elizabeth. She had a Cree father and a Shoshoni mother. Harmon intended to keep her until he returned to civilization; then he would, of course, leave her behind, under the protection of some honest man.

"The girl is said to have a mild disposition and an even temper," he wrote, "which are qualities very necessary to make an agreeable woman and an affectionate partner."

Three years later Elizabeth had a baby boy; Harmon named him George. The next year, at Fort Dunvegan on the icebound Peace River, Elizabeth had twin boys, born prematurely. They both died within a week.

When George was three, Harmon was stationed at a remote fort on the western slope of the Rockies in present British Columbia. He sent his son back to Vermont for an "English education." But a year later, soon after Polly was born, word came that George had died. Harmon and Elizabeth were devastated.

"When I informed her that our beloved son George was dead, she looked at me with a wild stare of agony and immediately threw herself upon the bed, where she continued in a state of delirium during the succeeding night."

They had a second daughter, Sally. In 1819 Harmon returned to civilization. He never considered his original intention of placing Elizabeth under the protection of some honest man. He and his thirty-year-old partner had shared too much joy and too much sorrow in their sixteen years together to now separate.

"We have wept together over the departure of several children," he wrote. "We have children still living who are equally dear to both of us. How could I spend my days in the civilized world and leave my beloved children in the wilderness? How could I tear them from a mother's love and leave her to mourn over their absence to the day of her death? How could I think of her in such circumstances without anguish?"

Harmon taught his daughters both English and Cree. He wanted his children to know their mother's language as a mark of respect for her.

The family traveled three thousand miles from western Canada to Fort William, the headquarters of the Northwest Company on Lake Superior. There, Elizabeth gave birth to another boy, John. Then they went on to Vermont.

But the Vermont natives did not welcome Harmon's Indian wife and her half-breed children. So Harmon and a brother founded a new town, Coventry, far to the north in the Lowell Mountains, where they would be safe from racial bigotry.

At first Harmon and Elizabeth prospered, and they had more children. Then hard times came and they moved back to Canada, to a small village near Montreal. Like many once-affluent fur traders, Daniel Harmon died in poverty. But he had always been loyal to his Indian-girl partner — the one he had originally agreed to take after the custom of the country.

Suggested reading: Walter O'Meara, *Daughters of the Country* (New York: Harcourt, Brace & World, 1968).

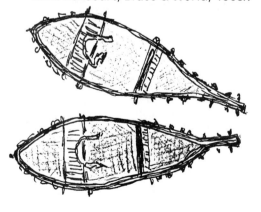
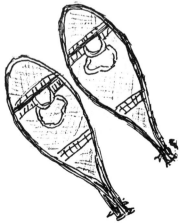

HAND TO HORN

Finan MacDonald, six feet four and broad across the shoulders, was a mountain of a man, but the buffalo he fought was a giant of a bull. Finan's wild red hair and bushy beard outshone the buffalo's. Finan's fist clutched the bull's top knot, keeping him away from the horns of the enraged beast.

Finan was a Gaelic-speaking Scotsman for whom English was always a second language. Many of the trappers watching the battle knew Finan well. They had traveled with him for most of the twenty years he had spent in the Canadian Rockies and the Pacific Northwest. Even they could not understand all the expletives which Finan molded from Gaelic, English, Blackfoot, and Flathead. But the air turned blue, and the spectators knew Finan was in good form.

Finan planned to retire to an Ontario farm. He had brought his Pend d'Oreille woman with him on this his last trip down from the mountains. Also with him was David Douglas, exploring botanist from whom the Douglas Fir got its name. In fact, you might say Douglas was how Finan got into this mess with the bull. They called it a hand to horn fight. Finan's was the most famous one in Canadian history.

Finan had wanted to retire the year before — in 1826. But the Northwest Company persuaded him to go out once more with the traps.

"We must seal off the Columbia country," company officials said. "If you can trap the land bare below the river it will keep out those upstarts, working up the Missouri and the lower Rockies. We need a buffer zone to preserve the Columbia for the British."

Douglas had traveled with Finan on that last trapping trip, adding to his impressive collection of botanical specimens. He persuaded Finan to transport his collection to a ship on Hudson's Bay.

Hunting had been good as they moved down the North Saskatchewan, past Fort Edmonton. On the last day of May, they saw a herd of buffalo. The next morning a hunting party killed two large bulls and wounded a third.

Finan helped the native hunters chase the wounded bull. But the animal suddenly turned on Finan. The Scotsman threw himself flat on the ground, hoping the bull would go on past and let him escape. But the bull lowered his head and hooked his horn into Finan's thigh. He ripped the leg open to the bone and threw Finan several yards into the air.

Douglas continued his description of the battle: "The wound

sustained was a dreadful laceration, literally laying open the whole back part of the thigh to the bone. He received five more blows, at each of which he went senseless. Perceiving the beast preparing to strike him a seventh, he laid hold of the wig and hung on; man and bull sank the same instant. His companions had the melancholy sensation of standing to witness their companion mangled and could give no assistance."

The bull and MacDonald lay together, two humps side by side on the prairie, for a long time. The hunters, out of ammunition, returned to camp for more bullets. The sun was down when they returned to the scene of the great battle.

"Be careful with your shot," Douglas said. "Finan may still have life in him, and you dinna want to hit him. Just one shot in the beast."

The shot aroused the bull. He struggled to his feet, "sniffed his victim, turned him gently over, and walked off."

Douglas ran up to the other lump, still motionless on the ground. MacDonald was alive, but unconscious. His wrist was dislocated. The worst injury was bruising to the left chest. Douglas thought Finan's shot pouch, filled with balls, shot and wadding, had saved his life. The bull's horns, penetrating the shot pouch, had broken two ribs right over Finan's heart.

Douglas trimmed and bound Finan's wounds. He wondered how long they would have to wait before his friend could travel, but Finan was tough. He had been one of the original English discoverers of the upper Columbia country in 1807, the year after Lewis and Clark left.

Finan MacDonald had not survived twenty years in the mountains by taking it easy. Even the ferocious Blackfeet feared him. After one battle with them Finan had reported: "Sixty-eight of the enemy remane in the planes as pray for the wolves. They will not be so radey to attack people another time."

Finan delivered Douglas and his collection to Hudson's Bay. Then he and his woman went on to Ontario to settle on a farm. Whites called the woman Peggy Ponderay. Finan married Peggy in a regular ceremony. By that time they had more children and some grandchildren. Peggy died in 1841 when she was about forty-three. Finan lived another ten years. He never adjusted to farm life.

Suggested reading: John Davies, *Douglas of the Forests* (Seattle: University of Washington Press, 1980).

BORN TO GUIDE

His mother has been honored through more monuments and memorials than any other woman in American history. In most of them she has a small child on her back, peeking over her right shoulder. Jean Baptiste Charbonneau is surely the most pictured mixed-race child — perhaps the most pictured of all children — in our nation's history.

His mother, Sacajawea, was the best guide Lewis and Clark had. One wonders if the ability was genetic. Charbonneau grew up to be a great guide, as well. In 1846 he guided the Mormon Battalion from Council Bluffs, Iowa, to San Diego, California, the longest military march in American history.

William Clark took a particular liking to Sacajawea's baby. He called him Pomp, and he named a prominent landmark on the Yellowstone River Pompey's Pillar after the child. Pomp's parents allowed Clark to raise Pomp as his own.

Clark hired tutors for his foster son. The boy enjoyed learning from books and soon became fluent in English and French. When he was eighteen Pomp met Prince Paul of Württemberg, who was on a scientific trip to the western United States. With Clark's consent, the prince took Pomp to Europe for the next six years.

The Prince, an excellent horseman and marksman, taught those skills to his young friend. He called his protege his "hunter extraordinary." Pomp continued reading and became fluent in several European languages.

It would appear that the Prince also learned something from Pomp. Just one step from being king of his country, Prince Paul once said this:

"In a palace I would feel like a wild thing that is imprisoned in a gilded cage. The ermine, the scepter, and the crown would be to me the emblems of a galley slave, and my heart would never cease to hunger for the vast silent places and the simple life among free unaffected children of nature."

The prince and Charbonneau returned to America in 1829. They went up the Missouri River to visit Indian villages, and then separated when the prince returned to Europe.

For the next fifteen years, Charbonneau trapped beaver and lived as a mountain man. He could talk in their own tongues with Americans, Frenchmen, Spaniards, Germans, and Indians from several tribes. His stories of overseas adventure added welcome variety to trapper tales told around campfires from New Mexico to Montana, to Oregon. He became well acquainted with trappers such as Jim Bridger, Thomas Fitzpatrick, Andrew Sublette, Joe Meek, Jim Beckwourth, and Louis Vasquez and with military commanders such as John C. Fremont, Philip St. George Cooke, and J. W. Abert. He guided William Drummond Stewart in some of his western trips. After he guided the Mormon Battalion to California, Charbonneau became Alcalde of San Luis Rey.

In 1839 Thomas Jefferson Farnham, New England lawyer traveling west, wrote about an educated Indian he had met near Bent's Fort. He gave no name, but Charbonneau was in the area. Here is what Farnham wrote:

"Why did you leave civilized life?" I asked.

"For reasons found in the nature of my race. The Indian's eye cannot be satisfied with the description of things, however beautiful may be the style or the harmonies of verse in which it is conveyed. I must range the hills, I must be able to out-travel my horses, I must always be able to strip my own wardrobe from the backs of the deer and buffalo, and to feed upon their rich loins; I must always be able to punish my enemy with my own hand, or I am no longer an Indian."

Considering Charbonneau's heritage and education, and the fact that he was in the vicinity, one suspects it was he.

By 1860 Charbonneau was a hotel clerk in Auburn, California. His good friend, Jim Beckwourth, found him there and stayed with him for a time. Charbonneau had apparently been in the area since shortly after the gold discovery in 1848. Some say he and Beckwourth mined as partners on the North Fork of the American River. Charbonneau had probably stayed in California after serving as Alcalde.

Sometime in spring 1866 Charbonneau and two companions left California for Montana. Charbonneau caught pneumonia on the trip and died near present Danner, Oregon. He is buried there, in a small, seldom-visited country cemetery.

All agree that Baptiste Charbonneau enjoyed the same popularity as an adult among mountain men, miners, and European royalty that he had known as a baby with Lewis and Clark.

Suggested reading: Ann W. Hafen, "Jean Baptiste Charbonneau" in LeRoy Hafen (ed.) *The Mountain Men and the Fur Trade of the Far West* (Glendale, Arthur Clark Company, 1965).

ORDERING INFORMATION

True Tales of the Old West is projected for several volumes.

Proposed titles include:

Warriors and Chiefs	In print
Soldiers	In print
Native Women	In print
Mountain Men	In print
Pioneer Women	In print
Ranchers and Cowboys	In print
Horses and Riders	Soon to appear
Frontiersmen	Soon to appear
Entertainers	Soon to appear
Writers	Under way
Scouts	Under way
Homesteaders	Under way
Dogs and Masters	Under way
Explorers	Started
Lawmen	Started
Outlaws	Started
Railroaders	Started
Merchants	Started

Ask at your bookstore or write:

PIONEER PRESS
Box 216
Carson City, NV 89702-0216